H. Wiley Hitchcock, editor

Prentice-Hall
History of Music Series

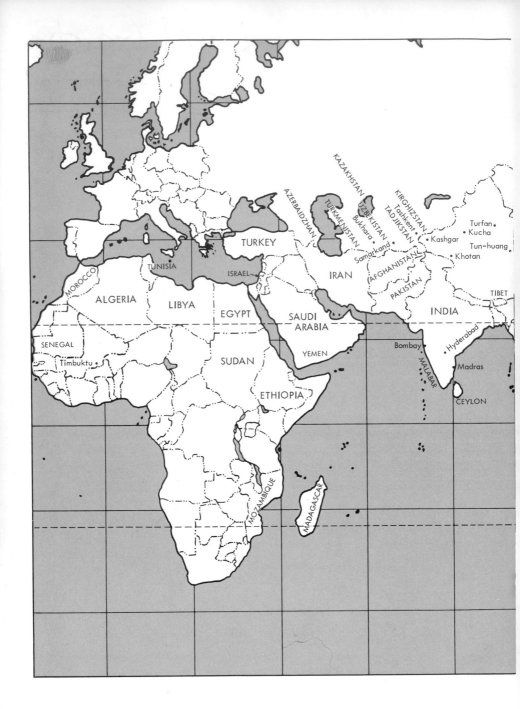

KAZAKHSTAN

KIRGHIZSTAN
Tashkent
TADJIKSTAN

AZERBAIDZHAN

TURKMENISTAN

UZBEKISTAN

Bukhara

Samarkand

Turfan
Kucha

Kashgar

Tun-huang

Khotan

TURKEY

IRAN

AFGHANISTAN

PAKISTAN

TIBET

TUNISIA

ISRAEL

MOROCCO

ALGERIA

LIBYA

EGYPT

SAUDI
ARABIA

INDIA

SENEGAL

YEMEN

Bombay

Hyderabad

Timbuktu

SUDAN

Madras

MALABAR

ETHIOPIA

CEYLON

MOZAMBIQUE

MADAGASCAR

Music Cultures of the Pacific, the Near East, and Asia

WILLIAM P. MALM

Professor of Music
The University of Michigan

PRENTICE-HALL, INC., ENGLEWOOD CLIFFS, NEW JERSEY

© 1967 by Prentice-Hall, Inc.
Englewood Cliffs, New Jersey

*All rights reserved. No part of this book may
be reproduced in any form or by any means
without permission in writing from the publisher.*

Library of Congress Catalog Card Number: 67-22089

Printed in the United States of America

C-60793-P

Current printing (last digit):
15 14 13 12 11

PRENTICE-HALL INTERNATIONAL, INC., *London*
PRENTICE-HALL OF AUSTRALIA, PTY. LTD., *Sydney*
PRENTICE-HALL OF CANADA, LTD., *Toronto*
PRENTICE-HALL OF INDIA (PRIVATE) LTD., *New Delhi*
PRENTICE-HALL OF JAPAN, INC., *Tokyo*

Foreword

Students and informed amateurs of the history of music have long needed a series of books that are comprehensive, authoritative, and engagingly written. They have needed books written by specialists—but specialists interested in communicating vividly. The Prentice-Hall History of Music Series aims at filling these needs.

Six books in the series present a panoramic view of the history of Western music, divided among the major historical periods—Medieval, Renaissance, Baroque, Classic, Romantic, and Contemporary. The musical cultures of the United States, Latin America, and Russia, viewed historically as independent developments within the larger Western tradition, are discussed in three other books. In yet another pair, the rich yet neglected folk and traditional music of

Foreword continued

both hemispheres is treated. Taken together, the eleven volumes of the series are a distinctive and, we hope, distinguished contribution to the history of the music of the world's peoples. Each volume, moreover, may be read singly as a substantial account of the music of its period or area.

The authors of the series are scholars of national and international repute—musicologists, critics, and teachers of acknowledged stature in their respective fields of specialization. In their contributions to the Prentice-Hall History of Music Series their goal has been to present works of solid scholarship that are eminently readable, with significant insights into music as a part of the general intellectual and cultural life of man.

H. WILEY HITCHCOCK, *Editor*

Preface

The purpose of this book is to survey the basic kinds of music and musical instruments found in the major oriental civilizations and in the island cultures of the Eastern Hemisphere. It also is intended as an introduction to the basic attitudes, techniques, and nomenclature of the discipline of ethnomusicology. These two goals are commingled, so that reading a given chapter provides preliminary information about the musical ways of one part of the world, whereas reading the entire book gives one an overview of the continuities and uniqueness in non-Western music, as well as a basic vocabulary with which to discuss music from any part of the world. Those general concepts not discussed in this book appear in Bruno

Nettl's companion volume, *Folk and Traditional Music of the Western Continents*, in this series.

Many musics from dozens of cultures and countries have been crowded into the following seven chapters. Our information is based on the writings of foreign and native authors of many professions; seldom are they musicians; they comment with varying accuracy on music as it seemed to them in their time. Our earliest authors come from ancient history, and our most recent are from the mid-twentieth century. Most of these authors had the advantage of hearing their music in its native setting.

The selected list of recordings at the end of each chapter will provide the reader with a channel to some of the same sounds, but it must be remembered that only a small part of the total musical effect can be ascertained by listening to the music alone. Where possible, background information has been provided so that the reader may place his listening in a proper cultural matrix.

Four basic approaches are used in this book: the anthropological, historical, organological, and musical. The anthropologist or behavioral musicologist looks at the place of music in culture, at the values a society attaches to it, and at the people who practice it. Historical musicology will be applied most often in literate societies such as those of India and China where historical periods and theoretical constructs were well established long before the monkish scholars of Europe "invented" the bases of Western art music. Archaeology will also help us in the reconstruction of historical data from destroyed civilizations as well as nonliterate societies. However, although the legends of the ancient and tribal worlds have some use to musicology, potsherds and burial mounds do not give the historical musicologist much to work with. They may prove useful, nevertheless, to the organologist, the student of the history and development of musical instruments.

Organology is important to this book, for many times the only information available in one area is a description of its instruments.

Such details tell us only a little about the actual music. When coupled with similar information from other areas, however, they can prove useful for studying possible diffusions of musics throughout the world. They also prepare the reader for what he should expect should he visit a given area in search of traditional music.

Whenever and wherever possible, we have been product musicologists; that is, we have looked directly at the musical sounds and tried to find out where they come from, how they make sense, and how one can learn to appreciate them. It is axiomatic that all musics do make sense, for they always consist of the disciplining of tones according to the aesthetic criteria of their particular time and culture. An understanding of such musical logics is the basic goal of this book.

Two major problems in preparing this book were transliteration and transcription. Most of the indigenous terms and instrument names mentioned are derived from languages which have more than one form of romanization. I have tried to choose that spelling for each term which is likely to be pronounced most closely to the original by the nonspecialist; I do not claim any linguistic consistency in my choices. Common alternate spellings are shown in parentheses. Transcription of non-Western music in Western-style notation always creates some form of distortion. To aid the reader in evoking the proper non-Western sounds I have, whenever possible, chosen my examples from recordings commercially available in the United States. Thus, the reader may use the transcriptions as guide lines and correct their inadequacies with his own ear. Special notational symbols are: (↑) a pitch higher than notated; (↓) a pitch lower than notated; (◡) a time slightly shorter than notated; (╱) or (╲) a sliding entrance to or exit from a note; and (♫) a series of pitches, with a slide from one to another. A note in parentheses is one that is barely heard. If the transcription is transposed, the approximate original pitch is shown at the beginning in parentheses. Any special symbols beyond these are explained in the examples using them. The examples are meant not only to illustrate specific points in the text but also to provide a variety of types for further analysis or discussion. Most appear in print for the first time. Unless otherwise noted, the transcriptions are my own. I wish to thank the many recording companies and publishers who have given their permission to make these transcriptions from their products. Full citations and credits are given below each example. Selected discographies and bibliographies appear at the end of each chapter. A map has been provided to help the reader locate unfamiliar places mentioned in the text.

Special thanks are due to Shigeo Kishibe, S. Ramanathan, Rulan Chao Pian, Hormoz Farhat, Barbara Smith, Mantle Hood, Robert Brown, William Hu, Ernest McCarus, Judith Becker, and Mark Slobin for invaluable information and criticism concerning their particular areas of specialization. Thanks go also to the Centers for Japanese, South and Southeast Asia, and Russian Studies of the University of Michigan for their cooperation in so many ways. Wallace Bjorke, Librarian of the University of Michigan School of Music, deserves special thanks for services beyond the call of duty, and Masakazu Kuwata is thanked for his excellent drawings. A special debt of gratitude is owed to H. Wiley Hitchcock for his dedicated and difficult work as editor. Finally, I thank those scholars who were willing to give advice but preferred not to have their names connected with a book in which one author attempts to cover such a vast area in so few pages. The information and judgments of this book are the author's own responsibility and do not necessarily reflect those of advisors and assistants named or unnamed. My hope is that the reader may find in this book the means to a broader understanding of music as a beautiful worldwide phenomenon.

W. P. M.

Contents

I

Australia and the Pacific Islands

Australian aboriginal music

A group of short, dark men painted with sacred markings of ostrich down and blood dance in a circle, holding each others' thighs. They leap like kangaroos while uttering animalistic shouts. What descriptive words come to mind? Stone Age, primitive, savage? All have been applied to the peoples of the Arnhem Land Aboriginal Reserve on the northern tip of Australia between the city of Darwin and the Gulf of Carpentaria. Among the earliest cultures still in existence, they are organized in bands, the simplest political units. Their society is a moeity; that is, every creature must belong to one of two basic clans (the *dua* and *jiritja*). Since aboriginals exist on forms of hunting, fishing, and food gathering that often involve moving with the wandering game, their material culture is minimal. "Common sense" would lead one to expect that their music would be rather pallid, yet field workers are unanimous in their praise of aboriginal songs. What is there to admire?

One of the first admirable aspects of Arnhem Land music is its meaningfulness to the culture. Music is used throughout an aboriginal's life to teach him what he must know about his culture, about his place in it, and about its place in the world of nature and supernature. As a baby he is encouraged to dance and sing about everyday tasks. At puberty he learns his first *karma* songs—about the totemic plants and animals of his clan and the history and mythology of the group—which belong to his lineage and have specific melodic formulas and modes that distinguish them from other groups' songs. In the bachelors' camp he learns more light-hearted songs which are the basic entertainment media for the band. When he marries and enters further into group responsibilities, however, it is the *karma* songs that are the central part of his education and his source of strength in times of trouble. His maturation can be measured in the esoteric knowledge he has acquired through song, and as an old man he knows that his honor is based partly on his mastery of the secret sacred songs of the band.

Nonliterate music in general shares this direct functionality with that of the Australian aboriginals. Literate civilizations, by contrast, tend to increase the separation of music from life. For example, a Western college student must learn to "understand" a Beethoven symphony. The aboriginal understands his music naturally. The Westerner can understand aboriginal music also, if he is willing to learn its language and laws and listen to it in terms of itself. It cannot be compared with a Beethoven symphony because it has nothing to do with it. Both, however, can be enjoyed once one knows what to listen for in each.

One of the first things to listen for in Arnhem Land music is the drone pipe, the *dijeridoo* (or *digeridoo*). This hollow eucalyptus branch is blown in such a manner that by back pressure and nasal breathing a constant tone is maintained. The pipe end may be placed in a large shell or can to aid the back pressure and the resonance. The instrument is stored in a stream or in mud to keep it moist and soft-toned. Some nine different tone qualities can be produced by a skilled player. The actual pitches played are usually two, a tenth apart. By alternating tone qualities and pitches the drone player produces a varied rhythmic and coloristic background for the singer, who will often work his melodic line against the drone in a manner reminiscent of Indian classical music.

A skilled drone player is highly respected and may travel with a professional songman to enhance trade meetings or other interband meetings. The songman himself may play rhythm sticks. For special occasions boomerangs are clashed instead. Beating on a log drum or on the side of the drone pipe is the only other form of native instrumental sound unless one includes the bull-roarer. This is an oblong wooden board that is spun overhead on the end of a string. Its sound indicates the presence of the supernatural, and women are forbidden to approach when it is sounded.

Arnhem Land music consists of sacred and secular songs, both containing secret and nonsecret pieces. In general there is little stylistic difference in the music though the accompaniment may change. The drone pipe pattern often helps to identify the songs in the *corroboree* meetings. Specific tunes, however, may be used for a variety of texts—just as, for example, Americans use the tune "John Brown's Body." This does not mean that there is only one style of music in Arnhem Land. Differences can be seen in the secular dance piece (a) and the song from an "all souls" ceremony (b) of Example 1-1. To speak intelligently about their distinctions, however, it is necessary first to learn certain rudiments of a non-ethnocentric music analysis—that is, an analysis in terms of the music itself rather than in terms of the ideals of one culture alone. These rudiments will be useful in the discussion of music from this and other music cultures.

Basic information in music analysis

One simple but important observation that must be made is the *performance practice*. Example 1-1a is performed by a singer with rhythm sticks plus a drone (shown here by only the first note). Example 1-1b is for singer and rhythm sticks alone. Both pieces use a solo singer. Whatever the mixture of singers and/or instrumentalists may be, it should be mentioned as a first step in describing a music.

Another observation has to do with *time*. Besides showing *tempo* in metronome marks and notating the rhythm of the sticks and its relation to the vocal part, one can note *meter*—that is, the organization of the basic pulse (*tact*) into units set off by accents. If these larger time units are the same length, as in Example 1-1, the piece is *isometric*. If the units are of equal length, but the individual unit is not a multiple of two or three (such as ⅝ or 1¼), it is an *asymmetrical isometer*. If the length of the units keeps changing (as in Example 4-1), the piece is *heterometric*.

The first few measures of both pieces in Example 1-1 seem to repeat a rhythm pattern. Since this deals with rhythm rather than meter, the phenomenon is known as *isorhythm*. It is very common in nonliterate songs as well as in Western art music. If there is no sense of a basic even pulse, the piece can be said to be in *free* rhythm. If the rhythms tend to follow freely those of speech, the piece is in *parlando-rubato* style. A steady tempo is called *tempo giusto*.

The effect of emphasis created by a change in the length of notes (for example, from short to long in 1-1b) is called an *agogic* accent. Finally, observations dealing with *rhythmic density* show the general increase or decrease in the number of notes.

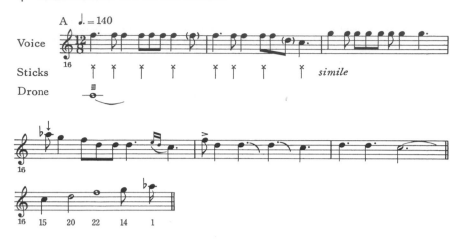

EXAMPLE 1-1. Two Australian aboriginal songs transcribed from the recording *Tribal Music of Australia* (New York: Folkways Record P 439), side 1, band 2 (second version) and side 2, band 6. By permission of Folkways Records and Service Corporation.

Several characteristics can be pointed out when *melody* is being described. Among these are: 1) the *scale*, 2) *pitch center*, 3) *range*, 4) *frequency* of notes, 5) prevalent *intervals*, 6) *cadence* patterns, 7) melodic *formulas*, and 8) *contour*. The first four observations can be made quickly by writing out the scale with all the notes used, including octave duplications if any, and assigning a large time value to the pitch center and progressively smaller time values to notes according to their frequency of use. (See the scale at the end of Example 1-1; numbers beneath the notes represent the number of occurrences in the melody.) This *weighted scale* method also shows the range. In describing scales, octave duplications are discounted (there are none in Example 1-1). Greek-derived terms are often used. Thus Example 1-1a is a *pentatonic* (five-tone) scale and 1-1b is *hexatonic* (six tones).

Though both 1-1a and 1-1b are only excerpts, one can show the frequency of intervals present in the following manner:

	Maj. 2nd	Min. 2nd	Maj. 3rd	Min. 3rd	P 5th
a:	5	1	0	3	1
b:	15	9	1	0	0

The cadence pattern for 1-1a consists of the notes D D C while that of 1-1b is a group of repeated C's. The examples are too short to speak significantly about melodic formulas, though extended patterns on one note are important in each excerpt.

Contour can be described in words—ascending, descending, pendulous, or terraced—or may be shown by graphic lines. Both pieces in Example 1-1 have basically descending contours.

Form cannot be analyzed in Example 1-1 since it contains incomplete pieces. In actual analysis, however, the term *iterative* can be used to describe a piece in which one small melodic formula is repeated throughout ("Clementine" is an example). If a piece returns to the original phrase after a digression, the form is *reverting* ("Swanee River"). If in either of these forms the same large formal unit is used for new text, the form is called, in addition, *strophic* ("Clementine"). If a form continues to add new melodic material, it is called *progressive*. These terms lose their usefulness when one deals with more complex musical structures.

In vocal music, another important characteristic is the relation of music to text. When one note is used for each syllable of the text, the style is *syllabic*. If one syllable is used with many notes, the style is *melismatic*. The study of text also offers opportunities for finding relations between language accents and music accents as well as musical reactions to important or colorful words in the poem.

While there is much more that one can do with music analysis,[1] these basic tools will help the researcher or the musically curious layman to understand a given music in terms of itself rather than in terms of one musical subculture of the Western world. I must add that only an innate musicality and an enthusiasm for finding beauty in sound will turn this knowledge into positive music appreciation.

Looking once again at the pieces in Example 1-1, we can see that analysis reveals their similarities and differences. They share an isometer,

[1] See further, Bruno Nettl, *Folk and Traditional Music of the Western Continents* (Englewood Cliffs, N.J.: Prentice-Hall, Inc., 1965).

an isorhythmic tendency, a descending contour, a related range (a sixth), and a stepwise melodic style. They differ in performance practice, tempo, scale, and cadences. Though the text is not shown, Example 1-1a is syllabic, and 1-1b is syllabic in the first half of each measure and melismatic in the second half. Space will not permit such lengthy analyses of each example in the book, but the format used here may prove useful to the reader in his own efforts at analysis.

Two excerpts from only two aboriginal genres show marked differences in style. What of the rest of the music? It is axiomatic of every culture mentioned in this book that if one took time to look further behind the musical aphorisms of this survey he would find an ever-expanding degree of sophistication and variety in style. Upon such detailed studies is founded the field worker's admiration.

In the midst of what appears, at first sight, to be a cultural desert we find many musical flowers. Recordings give us a bouquet of representative examples; however, as with real flowers, they are seen at best advantage in their natural setting. This is the reward of field work. Our pleasure will be vicarious, at best, as we skim among the islands of the Pacific.

Melanesia

North of Arnhem Land is New Guinea, the largest and least-explored island in the world. The great varieties of peoples who inhabit its mountains, jungles, and coastal plains range from Negroid Melanesians to Papuans and Pygmies. Its musical cartography has yet to be drawn, but already the music has revealed a vast and colorful range of styles.

One common performance practice in New Guinea is group singing in unisons or octaves. Such music is called *monophonic*. Sometimes one singer will sing a line that is answered by another singer or a group using the same or a different melody. This is *call and response* or *responsorial* and is common in New Guinea. If one group sings the call and another group sings the response, the performance practice is called *antiphonal*. But, regardless of the number of people involved, if only one melody is heard at a time the music is monophonic.

When many people are involved in a performance, the possibility of various notes appearing at the same time is great. Whether this is deliberate or accidental it is called many-voiced or *polyphonic* music. Polyphony occurs in three basic forms; harmony, counterpoint, and heterophony. If the different parts are performing different notes but in the same basic rhythm, this is *harmony* or *homophony* (see Example 5-3). If the different parts are performing different notes but are relatively independent rhythmically, this is called *counterpoint*. If the melodies of the various parts are related, this is *imitational counterpoint*. If they are basically the same tune but begun at different times, it is *canonic counter-*

point. One often finds the different parts performing the same tune at the same time, but each part presenting melodic or rhythmic variations. This is *heterophony* (see Example 3-1).[2]

The terms defined above form a basic vocabulary for describing music from any area of the world. However, it must be remembered that in any given piece the various techniques of polyphony cannot always be clearly separated. Example 1-2 contains elements of the types of polyphony that were previously described. After the caller (sometimes called the precentor) finishes his solo, the entire tribe enters in a manner that might be considered either heterophonic or a short moment of imitational counterpoint. The process is repeated in measure four, while measure six clearly illustrates native harmony.

EXAMPLE 1-2. New Guinea Polyphony transcribed from the recording, *An Introduction to the Music of New Guinea* (Bergenfield, New Jersey: Prestige International Record 25013), side 2, band 2. By permission of Prestige Records, Inc.

Although all forms of polyphony are found in New Guinea, the dominant style seems to be monophony. Vocal music predominates, often accompanied by hourglass-shaped drums (Plate I, figure 1). These drums are single headed and range from two to six feet in length. The open end

---

[2] Throughout these definitions the word "part" is used—rather than "voice"—because it may be applied to any music, instrumental or vocal.

of the drum is sometimes shaped like the open mouth of a crocodile or bird.

New Guinea drums are played primarily by male dancers, so there is often a handle at the waist of the drum which the dancer can grip in his left hand while pounding the skin with his right. The skin is that of a lizard or snake. It is attached with adhesive and tightened with a rattan hoop and heat. Human blood in the adhesive adds power to the drum, and small lumps of gum on the head give it resonance. The hoop is usually removed once the skin is set.

The hourglass drum and the songs it accompanies play a central role in the ceremonial life of New Guinea. For example, in the Hevehe, the long religious drama of Papua, constant musical accompaniment is required for every stage of the cycle, including the making of special houses, masks, and costumes beforehand as well as the actual ceremonial events. When this ceremony still flourished, it often took years to complete one Hevehe, for the entire cycle might stop for six months if a death occurred in the tribe and the resulting taboo on drumming was not lifted by one of the deceased's relatives. The drum was the symbol of the Hevehe dancer's power. It was relinquished by the dancers only at a final ceremony in which they were symbolically killed and their magnificent giant masks destroyed.

In New Guinea, as in Australia, one finds music pervading many aspects of daily life other than the ceremonial. Thus, there are songs for trading and war as well as for pig killing and puberty rites. Music is also used to establish the relations of individuals to their social matrix. Each family of the Kumaon tribe, for example, has a pair of flutes called *koa* which represent the tutelary spirits. An essential part of any boy's initiation ceremony is his introduction to the family flutes and the manner in which they should be played. In this way the flutes become concrete symbols of the nebulous but important concepts of lineage and familial continuity.

Such symbolism in music and musical instruments is common to most nonliterate cultures and is found in the music of many literate civilizations as well. The so-called masculine and feminine cadences of Western art music are an example. In New Guinea, the masculine-feminine idea is used to explain, among other things, the double rows of tubes found on some panpipes. Such an explanation is not merely fancy; it is a native form of music theory. The native has constructed his theory in analogies because, like the classroom teacher, he has found them to be an effective way of presenting abstract material orally. Of course, such analogies also lock music into meaningful relations with the things of value to him in his culture.

The important point here, however, is that the lack of music textbooks in a tribal society does not mean that its music is without a systematic base. It is, in fact, one task of the ethnomusicologist to look for the logic underlying each culture's music. In this hunt, the symbolisms and analogies of the native are often important clues to the structure of the system.

As implied earlier, the theory and symbolism of nonliterate music is part of the general "world view" (*Weltanschauung*) of a given culture and thus is best approached from the anthropological as well as the musicological point of view. For example, in studying the slit gongs found all over New Guinea, one must take into consideration the manner in which the large logs are hollowed out and slotted on one side so that the sound can come out, as well as the particular meaning of the various patterns played upon them. In addition, one must know the significance of the figures carved on a gong, especially in cases where one end of the log is stuck in the ground so that the carved head on the other end becomes a totem and the sound of the instrument represents the very voice of a god. Many large horizontal slit gongs are placed in special houses; the uses of these houses as well as the situations in which the gongs are used may reveal much about the people as well as about their music. Thus, an ethnomusicologist should be a man of many viewpoints if he is to appreciate fully the meaning of music in a given culture. The materials of one culture may in turn give one clues about broader musicological theories. For example, the panpipes of New Guinea and other parts of Oceania became grist in the Western musicological mill when the interval relations between the tones produced on them were found to be similar to the intervals of panpipes from such a distant area as the South American jungle. The resultant theory of overblown fifths (*blasquinten*) as expounded by Erich von Hornbostel (1877-1935) became a keystone in much of the construction of theories and controversies on the evolution of music.[3] For us, the panpipes form but another part of the battery of instruments created by the ingenuity of New Guinea artisans and musicians.

The same artisans have created another interesting instrument in the form of a bamboo trumpet. Its simplest form consists of a large bamboo tube closed at one end by a node in which a small hole has been made. Buzzing one's lips against this hole turns the tube into a trumpet. In its more complex form the bamboo trumpet consists of two vertical tubes connected at the bottom by a horizontal tube, at one end of which is a nodal mouthpiece, and by another horizontal tube connecting the two vertical tubes to form a square-shaped instrument. As in a French horn, the purpose of all these changes in direction is to produce the sound of a long horn with an instrument that occupies only a small space. Trumpets in New Guinea are used to frighten the enemy during battles and to signal the village of success when the warriors come home with the

---

[3] See Jaap Kunst, *Around von Hornbostel's Theory of the Cycle of Blown Fifths* (Amsterdam: Royal Institute for the Indies Mededeeling No. 76, Afd. Volkekunde No. 27, 1948). Another summary is available in Curt Sachs, *The Wellsprings of Music* (The Hague: Nijhoff, 1962), p. 102.

corpses of the foe. They are also used to enhance ceremonies. The same can be said for the bull-roarer, a common instrument throughout Melanesia.

We have emphasized a functional view of New Guinea musical instruments, but there are many instruments that are used primarily for self-amusement. Nose flutes, like the one shown in Plate I, figure 2, serve this purpose. Another common entertainment instrument is the jews'-harp or jaws'-harp. In New Guinea the jews'-harp is usually made of a short piece of bamboo in which a thin tongue has been cut. The wood is placed across the player's mouth and the wooden tongue is made to vibrate by plucking with a finger or jerking with a string. The player then creates a melody by changing the size of his mouth cavity. This type of instrument is found all over the world and is as much at home in its metallic form in the United States and Europe as it is in its bamboo form in Oceania.

Bamboo is used to make many other kinds of instruments in New Guinea, including rattles, beaters, and simple xylophones. It is even used to form a stringed instrument. Strips are cut along a bamboo tube in such a way that they are free from the tube along their lengths but still attached at both ends. When small wooden bridges are jammed under these strips they become tight and by plucking them a musical tone is produced. Since the strips are cut to different lengths and the bridges are of different sizes, a series of tones from which melodies can be played is produced. This tube zither looks like the *valiha* of distant Madagascar, although the strings of the latter are metal and are attached (as shown in Plate I, figure 3).

This survey of New Guinean music has revealed a full complement of percussion, wind, and even stringed instruments. The presence of polyphonic singing has also been noted, though the predominant style is monophonic. With all its variety, New Guinea exemplifies most of the major styles found in the other islands of Melanesia. To find the musical styles of the more famous Polynesian culture of Oceania we must move farther out into the Pacific.

Polynesia and Micronesia

The islands of the Pacific are scattered over such a wide area that one would expect to find a highly varied series of isolated cultures. However, a combination of amazing navigational skills and migrational incentives has bound the Pacific cultures in many ways. Our concern will be to point out common characteristics while drawing our examples from special regional forms.

Though our picture of Oceania today is one of tropical islands filled with lovely girls and easy living, the history of Polynesian societies is gen-

PLATE I. *Tribal Instruments*

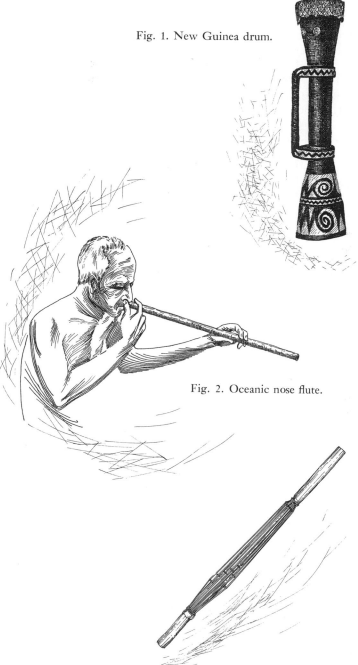

Fig. 1. New Guinea drum.

Fig. 2. Oceanic nose flute.

Fig. 3. Valiha (tube zither from Madagascar).

erally one of war and oppression. Strict caste systems have predominated, with the greatest supernatural power (*mana*) and the most *tabu* (or taboo) surrounding the aristocracy.

Before the entrance of European diseases, the Polynesians' greatest problem was over-population. The consequent needs for territorial expansion brought about extensive warfare. This warfare is reflected in some of the energetic posturing dances still done today throughout Oceania. One of the best-known dance traditions of Polynesia is the *haka*, done by the

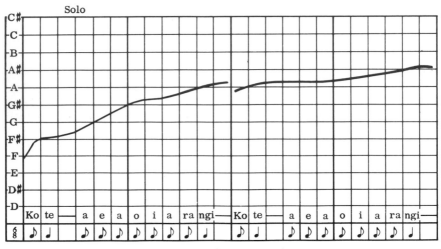

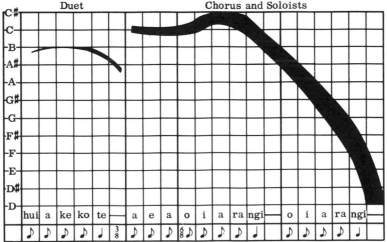

EXAMPLE 1-3. A Maori *haka* dance song transcribed from the recording, *Maori Songs of New Zealand* (New York: Folkways Record P 433), side 1, band 6. By permission of Folkways Records and Service Corporation.

Maori of New Zealand. As shown in Example 1-3, the music for these dances is sung in a style of declamation that lies between speech and song. This style is called *heightened speech*. The notation of such music is difficult, and some form of graph is preferable to the Western five-line staff.[4] Example 1-3 shows a typical *haka* performance practice in which the pitch rises as the leader calls out the main words and a chorus responds. Vocal sounds and various body percussions such as stamping feet, clapping hands, and slapping thighs help to keep the rhythm.

The concept of *whakaeke*—strict rhythm and a proper vocal unison —is very important to the correct performance of Maori music. Such concern is not merely a matter of aesthetics, because for the Maori to break the continuity of a song is to invite death or disaster. This is equally true in the more melodic *waiata* songs and in such reciting chants as the *patere*. The *patere* are of particular importance for they often deal with the history of the tribe or some personal genealogy. Chants concerning such matters may appear throughout Oceania, for the individual's place in the social and political structure of the entire society is largely determined by his family tree. In these preliterate societies, genealogical chants are the best way of keeping track of such complicated information. Thus, insistence on accuracy in the rendition of such chants and seriousness of musical training are important for the social position as well as for the safety of the performer from potential supernatural harm. Under such conditions, musical style should remain rather conservative and resist the influence of other musical cultures. Such is the case in some Polynesian groups.

Maori songs concentrate on a reciting tone called the *oro*. In the genealogical chants and similar forms of tribal historical chants, this tone is surrounded by tones of indeterminate pitch so that no specific scale system emerges. Even the more melodic styles that use specific, accurately sung notes may employ only three or four tones and use an iterative or progressive form. However, it should be remembered that such limited melodies serve primarily as memory aids in presenting the words. Such songs are listened to for the information they contain more than for a musically aesthetic effect. Because of the heavy word-orientation of such music, many songs are without meter or are heterometric, shifting accent to keep in step with the text.

In analyzing the tonal systems of Maori chants one often finds tones that do not fit within the tempered twelve tones of the Western scale. These "notes between the notes" are not mistakes. They are reflections of a different cultural concept of standard pitches. When one tries to notate these so-called *microtones* in Western, five-line, half-step-oriented notation, there is obviously a problem. This is sometimes solved by placing

[4] Important discussions of the various approaches to the notation of non-Western music are found in a symposium printed in the journal *Ethnomusicology*, VII, No. 3 (1964).

plus (+) or minus (—) signs or arrows (↑ or ↓) above the notes that are out of the Western tempered scale. Unfortunately, this system does not tell the reader how much higher or lower a given pitch may be. This problem was solved by Alexander Ellis (1814-1890) when he devised the *cents system*. He divided the octave into 1200 equal parts. One hundred of these divisions represented the standard Western tempered half step. If, therefore, an interval was 76 cents, its relation to the 100-cent half step or any other size of interval calculated in cents was easily seen.[5] Thus the cents system is an accurate comparative method of measuring intervals which in turn can be used to describe scales. If, however, measurement of an individual pitch is required, this is indicated by the number of vibrations per second since the cents system measures only intervals. Originally both cents and vibration measurements were made by ear with the aid of a device called a calibrated monochord. This consisted of a single string stretched over a board on which either cents or vibration figures were marked. The pitch of the string could be changed by moving a bridge along the calibrated board. The ethnomusicologist then tried to match the sound of his monochord with that of the musical tone in question. Today electronic equipment can be used instead, with much greater accuracy.

Not all Oceanic melodies are difficult to notate and describe tonally. There are many lyrical tunes. There also are various forms of pre-Western as well as Western-influenced harmonies. They appear in the form of drones, triads (three-note chords built in thirds), and occasionally preferences for fourths and fifths. Today one can hear missionary-hymn harmonies suspended over a drone with a chant-like melody above. When such foreign elements have been mixed with native elements the process is called *acculturation*. It is the basic state of Oceanic music today.

A good Oceanic example of acculturation in a musical instrument is the Hawaiian *ukulele*. It is a native version of a Portuguese mandolin that was introduced into Hawaii in the 1870's. Today its name is Hawaiian, the chords it plays are Western, and the tunes sung to its accompaniment are a mixture of both worlds.

The ukulele has a pre-Western ancestor called the *ukeke*. This instrument is a stick of wood to which are attached two strings that are raised from the wood by a bridge at each end. It was used primarily for evening serenading, and missionaries forbade its use.

In Hawaii, as in New Guinea, there are many other indigenous instruments, some of which are not readily described by Western analogies such as "native guitars" or "primitive clarinets." In the early twentieth century Hornbostel and Curt Sachs (1881-1959) proposed a method of describing and classifying all musical instruments in a scientific manner

---

[5] For specific instructions on how to use the cents system see Jaap Kunst's book *Ethnomusicology* (The Hague: Nijhoff, 1959), pp. 2-9, or Curt Sachs, *The Wellsprings of Music*, pp. 24-27.

that would avoid such ethnocentric analogies.[6] Let us illustrate the basic terminology of this system by describing the indigenous instruments of Hawaii with their proper scientific classifications.

The basis for classifying musical instruments under the Hornbostel-Sachs system is the material that creates the vibrations we perceive as sound; in this system there are five classes—*idiophones, aerophones, membranophones, chordophones,* and *electrophones.* The *ukeke* as well as the ukulele are classified as chordophones because their sound is produced by the vibration of a string. Actually, there are four kinds of chordophones. The *ukeke,* for example, is a *zither* because its strings are the same length as its sound board. The ukulele, however, is a plucked *lute* because its strings are parallel to its sound board and extend beyond it along a neck or finger board. The Western violin is an example of a bowed lute. The other two types of chordophones are not found in indigenous Polynesian music. They are the *harp,* with its strings at right angles to the sound board (see Plate XI, figure 33), and the *lyre.* The lyre's strings are suspended from the crossbar of a yoke and are parallel to its sound board.

Another instrument indigenous to Hawaii is the *puili,* split bamboo beaters now played in pairs. This is classified as an *idiophone,* an instrument whose sound is produced without stretching the basic material of which it is made. The gourd rattle *uliuli,* topped with feathers, is another Hawaiian idiophone; so is the *ili ili,* a double pair of smooth, lava pebbles that are clicked like castanets. The double calabash (*ipu*), which is hit on the sides and thumped on the ground, is also idiophonic. The *pahu* skin-head drum, however, is a *membranophone,* because its tone is generated by a vibrating membrane. Unlike the hourglass-shaped drum of New Guinea and its environs, the *pahu* drum is cylindrical. The sides of the cylinder are often carved into open lattice-work at the bottom so that the lower half of the body is a stand for the drum rather than a resonating part of the instrument. This form of drum and the hourglass type are the two typical forms found in Oceania.

A common form of wind instrument in Oceania is the nose flute (Plate I, figure 2), which in Hawaii is called the *ohe hano ihu.* It is classified as an *aerophone,* an instrument whose sound is caused by the vibration of a column of air. The conch-shell trumpet of Hawaii is also an aerophone, although the method of setting the air column in vibration differs. These differences are noted in the subclasses of aerophones. If the sound results from blowing across a hole, the instrument is a *flute* (end-blown or side-blown, depending on the position of the tube). If the air column is directed to a thin edge someplace below the point of mouth

[6] See Erich von Hornbostel and Curt Sachs, "Classification of Musical Instruments," translated from the original German by Anthony Baines and Klaus P. Wachsmann in *Galpin Society Journal,* 14 (1961), 3-29. A shorter version is found in Curt Sachs, *The History of Musical Instruments* (New York: W. W. Norton & Company, Inc., 1940), pp. 454-467.

contact as in a recorder or tonette, the instrument is a *block flute* or fipple flute. *Reed* aerophones use either single or double reeds that can be *free* (not touched directly by the lips) or *controlled* by lip pressure. If buzzing lips create the sound, the instrument is a trumpet or horn.[7] All forms of aerophones appear in Oceania. In Hawaii, however, only the flute and trumpet types are found. The former is played for self-amusement and the latter for signalling and for ceremonial effect.

The main use of Hawaiian idiophones and membranophones is to accompany the *hula*, the characteristic dance of Hawaii. In fact, many hulas are named after the instruments that accompany them, such as the *hula ilili* or the *hula puili*. Occasionally instruments are used in the main nondance form of Hawaii, the declamatory *oli* chants. As shown in Example 1-4a and b, these two forms reflect the typical chant styles of Oceania. The *oli* transcribed is practically a monotone and completely word-oriented in rhythm. The *hula*, by contrast, uses a three-tone (tritonic) scale, and the words are fitted into an isometric accompaniment on two drums. Note that even in such a restricted music the singer creates great variety by using ten different rhythmic versions of the first two beats of each measure while maintaining a continuity with the same rhythm for the last two beats in every measure except measure 16. Such ingenuity is easier to see in notation than to produce in performance. The art of the *hula* is by no means restricted to the gracefully symbolic and occasionally erotic movements of the dancers. Once again we see how the native musician displays the human talent for shaping musical materials in an interesting fashion.

EXAMPLE 1-4. An *oli* and *hula* chant transcribed from the recording, *Hawaiian Chant, Hula, and Music* (New York: Folkways Record FW 8750), side 1, bands 1 and 2. By permission of Folkways Records and Service Corporation.

[7] For further distinctions, see Sachs, *ibid.*

HULA

EXAMPLE 1–4. *Continued*

Our knowledge of Micronesian music stems primarily from a few early twentieth-century German studies in the Caroline Islands plus isolated German and American efforts before and after World War II. These materials reveal a predominantly vocal tradition which emphasizes the heightened speech or the litany chant styles. When it appears, harmony may be based on any interval, though movement in parallel fourths or the use of a drone are the most common. Most singing is integrated with gesture, whether the music be a lament, an invocation, or a serenade. A great deal of the music is used to accompany dance.

The musical instruments of Micronesia are few. The shell trumpet and nose flute are the most common, though standard flutes, jews'-harps, and even an occasional clarinet type are found. A common idiophone in Micronesia is a stick that is carried by men in certain dances. The performers strike each others' sticks in the course of the choreography. Indigenous stringed instruments are rare although one can find local imitations of ukuleles and guitars. Membranophones, likewise, are not common, though the hourglass single-headed drum shown earlier in New Guinea is found as far north as the Marshall Islands. In keeping with the ecology of atoll life, the skins of these drums are made of shark's belly or parts of the sting ray rather than lizards. There are many atolls without any indigenous musical instruments.

On the basis of present information and modern conditions, Micronesia presents the least developed musical culture area discussed thus far. However, it must be remembered that the value of this music is best judged by its meaning to a "culture carrier" rather than to a foreigner. For the men and women at a funeral who sing a repetitive lament filled with sliding indistinct pitches, there is great effect in the music, just as there is great release in singing a dance song even if it only uses three notes. The story a song tells or the poetry it supports may be ample reason for its being, even without its accompanying dance. Music in Micronesian culture today does not loom large in a world survey, but it serves important functions for the people who use it in daily life. One can only wonder what this music might have been like in the days of the great Pacific migrations.

Bibliography and discography

The bibliographies of Chapters 1 and 2 of Bruno Nettl's companion book in this series, *Folk and Traditional Music of the Western Continents* (Englewood Cliffs, N.J.: Prentice-Hall, Inc., 1965), cover many of the basic writings about the field of ethnomusicology in general. Of these, Jaap Kunst's *Ethnomusicology* (The Hague: Nijhoff, 1959) and its supplement are repeated here because of their extensive general bibliography of over five thousand items. Current bibliography is found in every issue of the journal *Ethnomusicology*. Bruno Nettl's *Theory and Method in Ethnomusicology* (New York: Free Press of Glencoe, Inc., 1964) speaks further of technical problems of field work and research, while Alan P. Merriam's *The Anthropology of Music* (Evanston: Northwestern, 1964) is the clearest statement of the behavioralist view of music.

In the specific area of Australian studies, the two basic works are A. P. Elkin & Trevor Jones, *Arnhem Land Music*, Oceania Monograph No. 9 (Syd-

ney: University of Sydney, 1957) and Catherine J. Ellis, *Aboriginal Music Making* (Adelaide: Libraries Board of Australia, 1964). Richard Waterman's "Music in Australian Aboriginal Culture," *Music Therapy* (1955), pp. 40-49, puts music in a social setting. Basic records are *Tribal Music of Australia*, Folkways P 439; *Australia and New Guinea*, Columbia KL 208; and *An Introduction to Music of New Guinea*, Prestige International INT 25013. F. E. Williams, *The Drama of Orokolo* (Oxford: Clarendon Press, 1940) discusses the Papuan drama cycle in anthropological detail, while Jaap Kunst, *A Study in Papuan Music* (Weltevreden, G. Kolff, 1939) deals with general tribal music. Johannes C. Andersen's *Maori Music with its Polynesian Background*, Memoir No. 10, supplement to the *Journal of the Polynesian Society* (New Plymouth, New Zealand: Avery, 1934) draws together important material from many old sources. It reveals the weakness of early drawings and transcriptions. Mervyn McLean's studies are more recent and reliable, as seen in *Ethnomusicology*, VIII, No. 1 (Jan., 1964), and IX, No. 3 (Sept., 1965). Modern examples of the actual music are heard in *Maori Songs of New Zealand*, Folkways FE 4433.

Robert Suggs' *The Island Civilizations of Polynesia* (New York: Mentor, 1960) provides an excellent background for Oceanic studies. Drawings of all known examples of musical instruments in Oceania are found in the back of Hans Fischer's *Schallgeräte in Ozeanien* (Baden-Baden: Heitz, 1958). Many of the Bernice P. Bishop Museum Bulletins such as No. 34 (*Polynesian Religion* by E. S. Handy) and Nos. 162 and 185 (*Southern Lau, Fiji* and *The Marianas* by Laura Thompson) contain references to music and dance. Bulletins 183, *Songs of Uvea*, and 109, *Native Music of the Tuamotus and Futuna*, by E. G. Burrows, and No. 29, *Ancient Hawaiian Music*, by Helen Roberts, are basic sources. *Hawaiian Chant, Hula, and Music*, Folkways FW 8750, is the best record.

2

The Philippines, Borneo, and Indonesia

The Philippines

The chain of islands that extends from Java through Borneo and the Celebes to the Philippine group contains a variety of cultural-historical influences as well as many indigenous developments. In this survey we shall start at the northeast end of the chain and try to point out some of the ways in which indigenous and foreign styles have interacted to produce a rich variety of musics and musical instruments.

If we look first at the remote tribes of the Northern and Central Philippine Islands we find that they share many traits with the peoples of Oceania. For example, Philippine tribes have a large repertoire of orally transmitted histories and mythologies which, like those of many Oceanic

peoples, are often sung in litany style with much use of sliding pitches. In addition, many instruments such as jews'-harps, end-blown flutes, nose flutes, and tube zithers are shared by these two areas. When one looks for more foreign influences, however, the two areas drift apart, for the dominant cultural forces in Philippine history were Spanish and Moslem.

The Spanish tradition has spread deep into the interior of the Philippines, where, for example, one can find the natives playing a small, four-stringed, plucked lute called the *kitara*, a word obviously related to guitar. Spanish influence becomes ever stronger as one moves towards Philippine urban culture. This can be seen in the standard *rondallas* bands of the rural villages and urban working-class districts. These bands consist of mandolins and guitars, often with bass viol and accordion added, and they accompany native dances whose choreographic roots are found in old Spanish quadrilles. Even the famous Philippine *tingkling* dance, in which the dancers maneuver between clashing poles, shows a mixture of cultural styles. The basic step is said to come from the movements of a native bird, but the arm positions and the musical accompaniment are truly Spanish.[1] Similar mixtures are found in such forms as the Tagalog *kumitang* pantomime dances and the *kundiman* sentimental ballads. Thus the general impression of urban and rural music from the Northern and Central Philippine Islands is that the dominant style of Philippine music is based on the social dances and popular music of nineteenth-century Spain.[2] If one moves towards the South, however, a very different music appears.

The dominant influence in the tribes of the South Philippines is Moslem. The primary source of this influence was post-fifteenth-century Indonesia. Therefore, one can expect to find musical parallels between these two areas. These relationships are most easily seen in the many non-Oceanic instruments found among the Moros and other southern peoples. The most obvious Indonesian influence is the *kulintang* orchestras of the Southern Philippines. These consist of sets of knobbed pot gongs (somewhat like figure 10) that are placed on racks and played in ensemble along with drums. Several layers of melody and rhythm are created in these ensembles in a manner very similar to the stratified parts of the Indonesian orchestras.

The Indonesian interest in xylophones is less evident in the Philippines, though the Magindanao peoples play melodies on a set of hanging wooden beams called a *luntang*, which forms what might be called a vertical xylophone. One also reads of natives breaking the monotony of a trip by playing melodies on two sticks tuned so that striking one against the other will produce different pitches. Another traveling instrument of more

[1] The relationship of this dance to similar forms found in Southeast Asia is of equal interest but belongs to the study called ethnic dance or ethnochoreology.

[2] A similar kind of compromise can be heard in the urban and rural music of South America, particularly from its western and northern coastal areas.

complexity is the *gitgit,* a small bowed lute with three strings that is often played by young men as they go courting. It is a diminutive version of the ubiquitous Moslem spike fiddle, known most commonly as the *rebab.* The *rebab,* in its original Near Eastern form, is believed to be not only the distant ancestor of the Philippine *gitgit* (via the Indonesian *rebab*) but also the predecessor of the bowed lutes of Europe, from the medieval *rebec* to the modern violin.[3] A belief in such a widespread relation of instruments is held by adherents to the *theory of diffusion,* which claims that every basic instrument type was invented only once and then spread about the world in variant forms. An opposing *theory of polygenesis* holds that each instrument was invented in several different places at different times. The variants of such separate inventions may or may not have overlapped as each form spread about. So far, neither theory seems to hold the exclusive answer to the questions of relationships between musical instruments around the world. One can find examples that seem to support each argument; however, the relation of the *gitgit* to the *rebab* certainly fits best within the concept of diffusion.

Another instrument of the Southern Philippines that seems closely connected to Indonesia is an end-blown notched flute with a rattan band tied around the top that helps to direct the stream of air. Its construction and playing method are those of the Indonesian *suling.*[4] A more complex relation between cultures is demonstrated by the Philippine *kudyapi.* This term is sometimes used generically for native-made plucked lutes, including a diminutive version of the guitar. The *kudyapi* important to this discussion, however, is a two-stringed plucked lute with five rather high frets. This instrument is sometimes called a boat lute because of its shape. It has many Southeast Asian relatives, such as the three-stringed crocodile zither (*mi gyaun,* Plate II, figure 6) of the Mon in Burma, the more abstractly shaped Thailand *chakay* zither (figure 7), the multistringed Javanese *kachapi* zither with movable bridges (figure 5), and the Borneo *kachapi, kasapi,* or *sapeh* (figure 4), which is a plucked lute with one to three strings that are played in the banjo position rather than horizontally as are the other instruments mentioned. The Philippine *kudyapi* is similar to the Mon and Thailand instruments in its physical characteristics and less like the Javanese and Borneo instruments; regarding its name, however, the reverse is true. This confusion of names and physical features illustrates the principle of *floating terms,* in which a word is transferred from one concept or instrumental type to a very different form as it moves from culture to culture or even within one culture over a period of time. It is important to note this phenomenon early in our study, because float-

---

[3] See Albert Seay's *Music in the Medieval World* (Englewood Cliffs, N.J.: Prentice-Hall, Inc., 1965), p. 73.

[4] Diffusionists would further connect it with the *nay* (*nai* or *ney*) of the modern Near East as well as the ancient Egyptian *sib.*

PLATE II. *Diffusion Examples from Southeast Asia*

Fig. 4. Kachapi from Borneo.

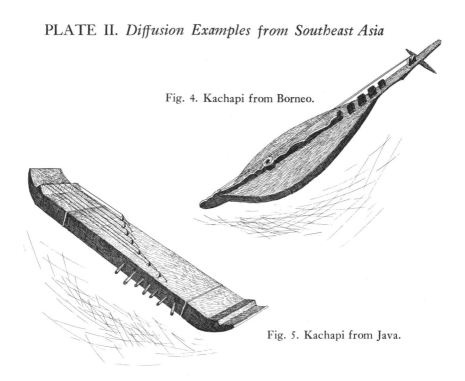

Fig. 5. Kachapi from Java.

Fig. 6. Mi gyaun from Burma.

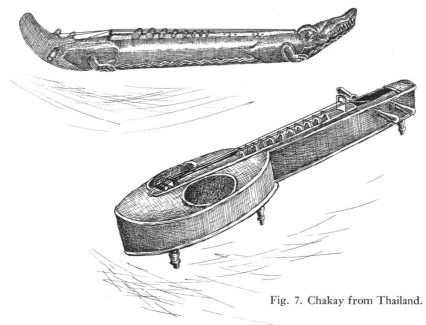

Fig. 7. Chakay from Thailand.

ing terms are so frequent that one cannot presume that the same term will mean the same thing when it is found in a new cultural context.[5]

Drawing on our discussion of influences and borrowings in Philippine music one must not think that this is basically a second-hand music tradition. The creative aspects of acculturation have been at work for centuries, and the modern ethnomusicological field worker as well as the nationalistic composers have found and are continuing to find rich stores of native music that reflect the many sides of the musical culture of the Philippines.

Music in Borneo

As one moves closer to the heartland of Indonesia by way of the islands of Borneo and the Celebes, the frequency of knobbed gongs, gong orchestras, simple xylophones, and end-blown flutes increases. This does not mean that all the music of the islands to the east of Java is Indonesian-derived. The Muruts of North Borneo, for instance, sing in an indigenous drone-based harmony unknown in Central Indonesia. We spoke of similar harmonies in Oceania and New Guinea. They also exist in isolated groups in Formosa and Southeast Asia, but no connection has been established as yet between these various systems.

Most of Borneo's melody and harmony is not based on Javanese scales but uses a five-tone scale without half steps, the so-called *anhemitonic* pentatonic (see Example 6-3). Though this scale is popular throughout East Asia, its use is so widespread even in other parts of the world that it cannot be said to prove connections between cultures. However, there is one instrument in Borneo that indicates a fairly clear link with the Asian mainland. It is an aerophone consisting of a gourd windchest holding several pipes, each of which contains a free reed. When holes on the pipes are closed, chords and melodies can be played. Such instruments are believed to be the oldest harmonic instruments in the world. They seem to have originated in Southeast Asia, probably Laos, and spread throughout East Asia. Thus, this tribal instrument of Borneo belongs to a chain of instruments that runs from the folksy *khaen* (Plate XI, figure 32) of Southeast Asia and China to the aristocratic *sheng* (Plate XII, figure 37) of ancient China and the *sho* of the Japanese court orchestra today.

These non-Indonesian examples from Borneo show that even in a seemingly isolated area a complex of influences can be absorbed into the current native style. It must be remembered that change is as much a part of a nonliterate culture as it is of the Western art-music world. Pure native or classical style is at best only a point in a cultural time continuum, albeit

[5] Those curious to follow such variants further should refer to Sibyl Marcuse, *Musical Instruments: A Comprehensive Dictionary* (New York: Doubleday & Company, Inc., 1964).

THE PHILIPPINES, BORNEO, AND INDONESIA 25

a lovely one. It can be stopped on a recording, but it inevitably changes in the living tradition. Thus, in Borneo one can still hear head-hunters chanting heterophonically over an ostinato played on a *sapeh* with the steady beating of a drum and a knobbed gong, or he can listen to another tribe singing the English words "bye bye" in indigenous-style harmony based on the pentatonic scale.[6] Both are native for the particular groups involved and for the particular time in which they are performed.

Field workers often feel that Western music has a pernicious influence on non-Western traditions, but if the non-Western culture carriers adapt it to their music, then the new musical resultant *is* the native style. When we turn to the main islands of Indonesia we can still find native traditions that have not yet succumbed to Western influence.

Indonesia—a historical introduction

The Indonesians were the last of four large groups of peoples to migrate to the Southeast Asian islands in prehistoric times. We know something of their culture from their many stone and metal artifacts as well as from commentaries written by the Chinese, who were in contact with Indonesia from at least the third century B.C. Indian influence and Brahman Hinduism entered Java in the first and second centuries A.D. Buddhism appeared in the fifth century and was particularly influential during the powerful eighth-century Sailendra Dynasty. Brahmanism remained in parts of the empire and eventually returned to the central courts where it merged with Buddhist and indigenous cult traditions. Trade and conflict brought various Indonesian empires in contact with the Chinese, Mongol, and Arab worlds. Mohammedanism was present in Indonesia by at least the thirteenth century and was quite prevalent by the fifteenth century. Portuguese, Dutch, English, and other Western influences have increased steadily since the sixteenth century. This long line of cultural contacts has helped to create the rich mixture of musical styles found in Indonesia today and, as we pointed out, possible relations may be found between the musics of the ancient high civilizations of Java and those of other native cultures along the Southeast Asian chain.

The gamelan

The center of the art music tradition of Indonesia is the Javanese *gamelan*, a generic term for orchestra. This orchestra may vary in size from a few instruments to over seventy-five. In *gamelan* music three basic functions are served, regardless of the ensemble's size. First, a basic melody

[6] Compare band 1, side 1, of *Borneo* (Paris: Contrepoint MC 20.112) with band 4, side 2, of *Murut Music of North Borneo* (New York: Folkways FE 4459).

is played in a relatively slow, unadorned fashion, somewhat like a Western *cantus firmus*. Secondly, many layers of elaboration are constructed around this nuclear theme. Finally, a set of interpunctuating gongs is used to divide the melody into various temporal sections. We shall discuss the *gamelan* instruments in relation to these three functions.

The basic melodic instrument is the *saron* (Plate III, figure 9), an idiophone with bronze keys set over a box resonator. It is played with a wooden mallet. As each new note in a melody is played the previous one is dampened with the thumb and forefinger of the left hand. In this way the melody emerges clearly.

The *saron* comes in three sizes. The highest and smallest is called the *saron panerus*, the middle is the *saron barung*, and the lowest is the *saron demung*. Generally speaking, the larger and lower the instrument, the fewer notes it will play. For example, usually the *panerus* plays the theme in repeated notes while the *barung* and *demung* play the melody in its purest form, as shown in Example 2-1.

The degree of complexity in the elaborating (*panerusan*) parts varies with the instrument and the particular piece. Three sizes of *bonang*, sets of bronze knobbed horizontal gongs placed on ropes in a wooden frame and played with two padded sticks (Plate III, figure 10), play variations on the theme. The wooden-keyed, box-resonated *gambang kayu* xylophone paraphrases the nuclear theme with rapid passages. Its two thin sticks with padded disks sometimes play independent lines as well as octaves.

The two-stringed, bowed *rebab* (Plate III, figure 8) and the end-blown *suling* flute ornament the melody, as does the *chelempung* zither. The latter has 26 strings tuned in double courses—that is, adjacent pairs of strings are tuned to the same pitch, giving a total of 13 tones.

The best-known elaborators are the *gender barung* and its counterpart, tuned an octave higher, the *gender panerus*. There is also a lower, single-octave form called the *gender slentem* or *panembung* (Plate III, figure 11). A *gender* consists of a series of thin bronze keys of fine alloy suspended by strings over individual tube resonators. The playing sticks terminate in padded disks. The combination of key, resonator, and beater produces a mellow, nonpercussive sound. Stopping this resonant tone is a problem, particularly on the *gender barung* where two hands play separate elaborating parts. This is solved by a supple wrist action that allows the player to stop the last note played with a finger or the side of his hand, while playing the next note. The highest pitched *gender panerus*, although it plays twice as fast as the *gender barung*, is considerably less difficult to master technically. The lowest pitched member of the family, the *gender panembung* or *slentem*, usually plays the theme or anticipates it.

While the nuclear theme is the point of orientation for all these strata of elaboration, the anchor for the entire ensemble is the *colotomic* structure. A colotomic structure is any system that marks off music into

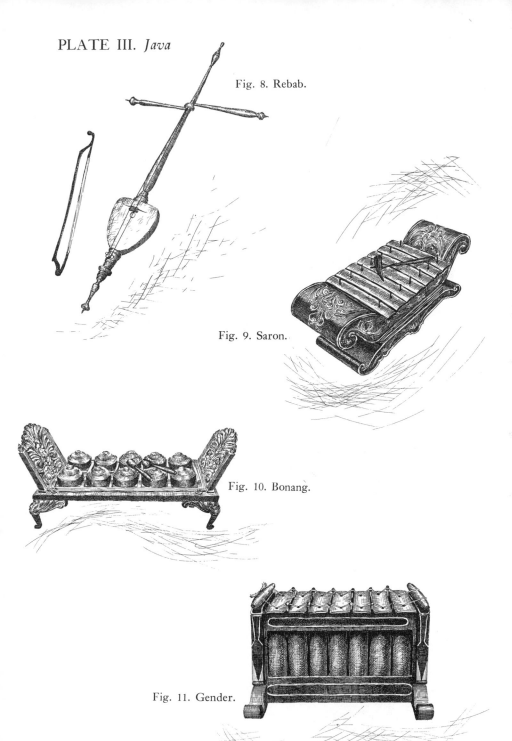

PLATE III. *Java*

Fig. 8. Rebab.

Fig. 9. Saron.

Fig. 10. Bonang.

Fig. 11. Gender.

EXAMPLE 2-1. A *gamelan* excerpt derived from Jaap Kunst, *Music in Java* (The Hague: Nijhoff, 1949) II, 483-484. Used by permission.

EXAMPLE 2–1. *Continued*

temporal units by the entrance of specific instruments in a specific order at specific times.

	1	2	3	4	5	6	7	8	9	10	11	12	13	14	15	16
ketuk	x		x		x		x		x		x		x		x	
kenong			x				x				x					x
kempul					x				x				x			
gong																x

EXAMPLE 2-2. A typical Javanese *gamelan* colotomic structure.

In Java, this generally consists of four levels of gong rhythm. In a standard sixteen-beat phrase the levels would be as shown in Example 2-2. The smallest, horizontal knobbed *ketuk* gong plays most frequently, the larger horizontal *kenong* is next, the hanging *kempul* plays only three times, and the big *gong ageng* plays but once. These four rhythms combine in the knowledgeable listener's ear into a progression of punctuations that leads inevitably to the cadencing gong. The word for melodic phrase in Java is *gongan*, for the entrance of the gong's beautiful, ponderous sound represents the completion of a thought as well as the end of the colotomic substructure on which it rides. In this sophisticated art music there are often changes in the colotomic structure and its relation to the nuclear theme, but a basic understanding of the logic of Javanese music must always begin with these two fundamentals.

There are two basic kinds of *gamelan* playing in Java, the loud style with an emphasis on the bronze instruments, and the soft style in which the flute, *rebab*, and *chelempung* zither may appear.[7] In soft style the *rebab* player is the leader, while in loud playing he is replaced by a drummer who performs on the double-headed *kendang*. Solo and unison chorus singing is also frequent in *gamelan* music and is an important vehicle for Javanese classical poetry. More intimate settings of such poetry are found in the various chamber music ensembles of Indonesia. A good example of such a group is a trio found in Sunda (West Java) consisting of a singer, a *suling* flute, and a *kachapi* zither (Plate II, figure 5). The zither has from six to eighteen strings that are tuned with terminal pegs and movable bridges. An interesting aspect of the music of this small ensemble is that the three musical functions found in large *gamelan* are still present.[8]

Among Indonesia's vocal forms one must include *krontjong*, a modern popular music based on models derived from sixteenth-century contact with Portuguese sailor's songs. However, the bulk of Indonesian literature, as exemplified by the tales of the hero Pandji and the local versions

[7] Compare this with the two styles of orchestra in Southeast Asia discussesd in Chapter 5, pp. 91-96.

[8] This can be seen by studying Appendix 53 in Jaap Kunst, *Music in Java* (The Hague: Nijhoff, 1949) II, 537.

of the Hindu *Ramayana* and *Mahabharata*, is carried through the oral tradition of the theatre, solo songs, and the orchestral literature. Of particular importance is the reciting of the *dalang*, the chief operator of the *wayang kulit* puppet theatre. Thus, the majority of Indonesia's literature is intimately connected with the art of music. We noted a similar connection in Oceania and will find further examples in many cultures of the Near East and Southeast Asia.

The Javanese tone system

There are two basic scales in Java, the five-toned *slendro* and the seven-toned *pelog*. A study of the fixed tunings of the keys from the *sarons* and *genders* of many gamelans throughout the island indicates that there is great variety in the actual pitches of, and intervals between, the notes of these scales.[9] The *slendro* scale is particularly varied. Example 2-3 shows a typical (note, *not* a standard) *pelog* and *slendro* tuning with the intervals marked in cents[10] compared with an idealized Western tempered scale of one hundred cents to the half step. The Javanese terms for the notes of the scale are given below each pitch.

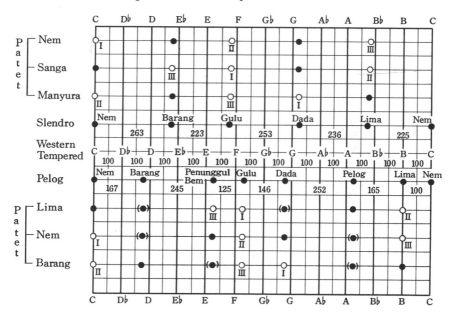

EXAMPLE 2-3. The Javanese tonal system.

[9] An attempt to explain this variety is found in Donald Lentz, *The Gamelan Music of Java and Bali* (Lincoln, Nebraska: University of Nebraska, 1965).

[10] The specific intervals chosen are derived from the measurements for *gamelan* number 5 in Appendices 61 and 62 of Jaap Kunst, *op. cit.*

Each tuning system has three modes called *patet*. These are shown in the upper and lower portions of Example 2-3. Each *patet* has a different set of principal tones that receive special melodic and colotomic emphasis. These are indicated in Example 2-3 by circles and the Roman numerals I, II, and III. For example, the *slendro patet manyura* uses the tones *dada* (near the Western G), *nem* (near C), and *gulu* (near F) as principal tones. Note that these tones stand in a fifth relation, in the Western analogy F-C-G. The specific tunings given in Example 2-3 show that the Indonesian fifths are not the same size as the standard Western form (702 cents) nor are they equal to each other. These differences make the so-called *slendro* and *pelog* fifths very important as principal intervals in the building of melodies within each *patet*.

The *pelog* tuning system contains seven tones, but only five are considered essential to each *patet*. The auxiliary tones vary from *patet* to *patet*. They are shown in parentheses in Example 2-3.

In performance a *patet* may be identified by special introductory and cadencing melodic patterns appropriate to it. In addition, each *patet* is associated with special times of the day and periods in the formal divisions found in the performance of Javanese theatre. Such extra-musical connotations for modes are common throughout much of Asia.

The relation of tone systems to theatre brings up again the subject of the function of *gamelan* music. We have already mentioned its basic function, the accompaniment of dancing and drama. These theatrical arts may be executed by either actors and dancers or by doll or shadow puppets. In the latter case, the ensemble tends to be more intimate in order not to cover up the dialogue of the *dalang* puppeteer. *Gamelan* music is also used in important religious and secular ceremonies. Many *gamelan* are privately owned. There are also amateur as well as professional musicians. Traditional teaching is by rote although native notation systems exist. The schools of *gamelan* playing founded after the independence movement following World War II have placed a greater emphasis on notated parts so that the improvisatory skill of the younger musicians has been seriously weakened.

Throughout Indonesia there is an endless variety of *gamelan* including some whose instruments are made of iron or bamboo. The bamboo instrument called the *angklung* is of particular interest. Each *angklung* consists of two or more bamboo tubes tuned in octaves and hung from a frame above a slotted tube in which the ends of the tuned tubes are suspended. When shaken, each *angklung* produces one pitch at as many octave intervals as it has additional tubes. In order to play a melody it is necessary to have as many players as there are tones in the scale used by that melody. Each player shakes his *angklung* in a different rhythm in order to produce the melody. A tune that is created in this manner by the interlocking of several different tones or short melodic fragments is known as a *resultant* or *composite melody*.

Balinese music

The most famous variant orchestra in Indonesia is the Balinese *gamelan*. The generally sedate quality of Javanese music is completely shattered by the boisterous brilliance of the Balinese sound. In Bali, instruments similar to those of the Javanese *gamelan* are found performing analogous functions. However, the Balinese *gender* and *gangsa* (the equivalent of the Javanese *saron*) are built in pairs or quartets in each octave size. While all the instruments in a set are in the same scale, half are "female" instruments, which are tuned lower than their "male" companions. When the two groups are played together they create a shimmering throb because of the beats caused by their tuning differences. This lovely sound is characteristic of the Balinese ensemble.

Among the several instruments that elaborate on the nuclear theme (in Balinese *pokok*) is the *trompong*, a two-octave set of ten knobbed gongs. Unlike the two rows of gongs in the Javanese *bonang*, the *trompong* gongs are in one row. They are played with the greatest flourish, and the performer's movements seem to be almost dancing. The Balinese colotomic instruments are similar to those of Java, with the addition of small cymbals. The softer *rebab* and flute sounds are less important, and there are two drummers instead of one. In addition, there is often a *reyong*, a set of twelve gongs placed in a row and played by four men. They produce rippling, elaborating resultant melodies by the interlocking of their parts.

The principle of interlocking parts is very important in Balinese music. The two drummers play complementary rhythms that result in one very complex line. The *gender*, and sometimes the *gangsa*, also exploit this technique. Example 2-4 shows two short *gender* excerpts, a *reyong* pattern, and their resultants. Those who know Western music history will recognize this as a more sophisticated version of the old European hocketing technique. The creation and perfection of these resultant melodies is one of the delights of Balinese performers.

In Bali, performers are also in a sense composers because, while one man may create the nuclear theme, he will receive suggestions from the players as he teaches them by rote their various elaborating parts. This group composition method points up the communal aspect of the *gamelan*. Most Balinese *gamelan* are clubs organized within a ward or village. Part of their vitality stems from their democratic base as well as their thorough integration into the social and ritual life of the community.

Another reason for the *gamelan's* survival in the modern world is the fact that its musicians have remained creative. New pieces and new styles of playing are constantly being developed. An individual piece remains only relatively unchanged once it is set. It does not become a fixed, sacrosanct "classic." Some pieces may disappear when new ideas come to the

EXAMPLE 2-4. Balinese resultant melodies derived from Colin McPhee, "The Five-Tone Gamelan of Bali," *The Musical Quarterly*, XXXV, no. 2 (April, 1949), examples 19 & 21, pp. 274, 275. Used by permission.

musicians, new dances are created, or the people simply get tired of the piece. Thus the Balinese music and dance world offers a refreshing mixture of traditional and indigenously new art forms.

Conclusion

Despite the many new musical experiments found all over Indonesia, one can still hear traditional sounds such as a quartet of *gender* subtly accompanying an all-night puppet play, a sedate chorus and orchestra performing for a Javanese court dance, or the overwhelming crash of a Balinese *gamelan* playing the entrance music for a witch or a sacred animal in a dance-drama. Such musics are pleasing to the ear, and the theoretical systems that govern their structure are fascinating to the intellect. These admirable features are all the more impressive when one remembers that the high level of artistic ensemble playing needed to perform such music is maintained by rural as well as urban populations. If we look back over the entire string of cultures surveyed in this chapter, it should be evident that between the village gong ensembles of the Philippines and the court orchestras of Java there is truly a host of wonderful musics available to the listener who will seek them out.

Bibliography and discography

Professional Philippine music studies are rare. A preliminary summary is Norberto Romualdez's "Filipino Musical Instruments and Airs of Long Ago" in *Encyclopedia of the Philippines* (Manila, 1934) IV, 86-128. The best recent research has been done by Jose Maceda, whose writings are found in *Ethnomusicology* (May and Sept., 1958) and in his dissertation, *The Music of Magindanao in the Philippines* (Ann Arbor: University Microfilms, 1964). The latter is coordinated with the Folkways recording *Music of the Magindanao* (FE 4536). Another good recording of native music is provided by Maceda and Folkways in *Hanunoo Music from the Philippines* (FE 4466). Urban popular music in the Spanish style is heard in Folkways record *Folk Songs of the Philippines* (FW 8791) and professional *rondalla* playing on the Monitor record *Bayanihan* (332). The Folkways record *Murut Music of North Borneo* (FE 4459) illustrates native harmony and some instruments. The Dayak tribal music is heard on the French Contrepoint record *Borneo* (MC 20.112).

Jaap Kunst (1891-1960) was a prolific and master scholar of Indonesian music. His *Music in Java* (The Hague, Nijhoff, 1949) in two volumes is a classic. Mantle Hood's *Patet in Javanese Music* (Groningen: Wolters, 1954) is a detailed study of modal problems, and his article "The Enduring Tradition" on pages 438-560 of *Indonesia* (Ruth McVey, ed., New Haven: HRAF Press, 1963) places music in its cultural and theatrical matrix. Colin McPhee's definitive study of Balinese music is *Music in Bali* (New Haven: Yale University Press, 1966). His *A House in Bali* (New York: The John Day Company, Inc., 1946) gives a charming picture of the place of music in Balinese life. Walter Spies and Beryl de Zoete show the riches of Balinese theatrical life in *Dance and Drama in Bali* (London: Faber & Faber, Ltd., 1938). Studies of other islands are found in Jaap Kunst, *Music in Flores* (Leyden: Brill, 1942) and *Music in Nias* (Leyden: Brill, 1938). The Decca album *Music of the Orient* (DL 9505-06) contains old recordings of both Javanese and Balinese music. Folkways' *Music of Indonesia* (FE 4537) has a broader selection, as does Kunst's Columbia Masterworks album *Indonesia* (KL 210). The Columbia *Dancers of Bali* (ML 4618) records the repertoire of the Pliatan *gamelan* on its American tour, and Columbia's *The Exotic Sounds of Bali* (ML 5845) illustrates how Western students from the Institute of Ethnomusicology at U.C.L.A. can play "foreign" music with skill and taste.

3

Moslem Africa
and the Near East

Negro Africa

Indonesian-African comparisons—Madagascar and Mozambique. Although the geographic distance from Indonesia to Africa is great, the cultural ties are clear. For example, on the African island of Madagascar the oldest culture, Malagasy, is Malayan, and its language belongs to a Malayo-Polynesian stock closely related to the speech of South Central Borneo. Musically, Madagascar has at least two instruments reminiscent of Indonesia—the *valiha* tube zither (Plate I, figure 3), with twelve to eighteen metal strings, and the *jejo vaotavo* stick zither, with from four to twelve strings. The latter looks much like the Southeast Asian model shown in figure 34 of Plate XI. Both these instruments are used by secular bards. The *valiha* is also found in French-African popular music ensembles, often combined with a guitar and bass. This tube zither is commonly made to sound louder by placing one end of it on an empty gasoline can. Unlike its Asian counterparts, the *valiha* also exists in a boat-shaped case zither form. In either form, the *valiha's* use of diatonic scales and parallel (organal) harmony in thirds is derived from Africa, not Indonesia.

Madagascan primitive xylophones, consisting of sticks of wood placed over the legs of the seated player, may also point toward an Indonesian inspiration. However, many non-Indonesian instruments like the Arab bowed chordophones of the *rebab* and violin family, and the French military drums, flutes, trumpets, and clarinets can be found in Madagascar. These instruments may be combined in many ways to accompany the open air *hira-gasy* theatricals. Such performances consist of music and dance plus long moral songs or proverbial speeches. In some parts of the island, Western drums and flutes have become essential parts of otherwise purely native funeral ceremonies.

If we return to our comments on possible Indonesian-African relationships, further examples can be found on the Southeast African coast. The Chopi tribesmen of Mozambique play extended dance suites (*ngodo*) with large orchestras of many-sized xylophones called *timbila*. These instruments have wooden keys and gourd resonators which, like other resonated African xylophones, have a sound hole thinly covered with a membrane to produce a characteristic African buzzing sound. The poems used in the Chopi suites are topical, not classical as in Java; nevertheless, the *gamelan* concept seems to hover in the background. There have been attempts to show even further relations with Indonesia through the study of xylophone tunings among the Chopi and in more distant parts of Africa. However, the most common shared traits of these two areas are found in the musical legacies of Mohammedanism, for Africa and Indonesia are at two ends of an Islamic cultural stream. This stream is generated centrally in the Near East rather than flowing directly from East to West or vice versa, and it is this Islamic influence on Negro Africa that offers the most fruitful comparative material.

The Islamic influence on Negro African music

In Africa, Islam extends over much of the Hamitic and Nigritic areas of the East coast, across the Mediterranean littoral, and down through West Africa to the fringes of the Sahara. Wherever it appears, the local musical style is affected.

In Negro Africa the musical changes caused by Moslem influence are rather specific and easy to identify.[1] Negro Moslem singers will ornament

[1] For a discussion of other Negro African styles, see Bruno Nettl's *Folk and Traditional Music of the Western Continents* (Englewood Cliffs, N.J.: Prentice-Hall. Inc., 1965).

their lines with quick, microtonal shakes and mordents. They tend to use a tense, nasal voice quality. When voices and instruments are combined, the accompaniment is not the multiple drums or ostinatos on a melodic instrument as found in Central Africa, but rather a single or double drum (often of a kettle, hourglass, or frame-drum type) or a bowed stringed instrument (like the *rebab*) playing heterophonically. In general it seems that the polyrhythms of pagan Africa give way to single rhythmic lines wherever Islam has become dominant. In addition, the several harmonic and contrapuntal traditions of pagan Africa become less prominent under Moslem culture, for in general Moslem music tends to be monophonic though heterophony and drones can also be found. Finally, Moslem influence is seen whenever a double-reed instrument appears in Africa.

The acceptance of Islam does not necessarily mean the total destruction of indigenous traditions. At the terminals of the Sahara caravan routes, there are many Negroid groups that either maintain two separate musical traditions or show a mixture. The Wolofs of Senegal and Gambia, for example, show a mixture. They use cylindrical and pot-shaped, single-headed drums in groups to produce African polyrhythms for their secular dances. When, however, their holy man sings Moslem hymns (*hasida*), a small kettle drum called a *tabala* is used, along with an iron beater. Together they produce simple, single rhythms much more akin to the music of the rest of the Moslem world.

Wolof society has a class of professional entertainers (*gewel* or *griots*) who, in keeping with both Negro and Moslem traditions as well as those of many other cultures, are considered to be lazy, boisterous, and of low class.[2] Nevertheless, they are well paid, for music is an essential, functional part of many phases of African life, just as it is in Oceania. The performances of these musicians reflect a Negro-Moslem mixture, for they sing praise songs—a common pagan African genre—with tense North African voices. They also tell stories to the accompaniment of a plucked five-stringed *halam*. The narrative traditions which they use are as old as the camel caravan routes of Moslem and even pre-Moslem Africa. However, while the Moslem caravan narrators bowed heterophonic accompaniments to their tales, the Wolofs play plucked, drone-like harmonies. Similar mixtures of styles can be found all along the fringes of the Sahara.

In the Sudan and Ethiopia, where the racial mixture is extensive, a great variety of bowed lutes and monophonic songs is found, as well as lyres that recall the more ancient cultures of Egypt. In Ethiopia, the situation is further complicated by a strong Coptic Christian tradition, not to mention the Falasha Jews. The Copts use stone bells (*dowel*) and sing in a melismatic chant style that intrigues the ear with its Christian-Moslem

---

[2] For a discussion of the curiously consistent low position of musicians in world societies, see Alan P. Merriam, *The Anthropology of Music* (Evanston: Northwestern, 1964), Chapter VII.

mixture. An excellent illustration of the manner in which such traditions can combine can be heard on the Ethnic Folkways record *Folk Music of Ethiopia* (FE 4405, side 2, band 2), in which a nasal-voiced singer is accompanied by a Moslem spike fiddle while performing a Negro-style praise song in honor of his Christian king. Such are the dynamics of acculturation.

While other African groups show unique variations in their acculturation of musical styles, the general principles stated above give some indication of the directions that Negroid African music may take under Moslem influences. Our look at an Ethiopian example actually led us beyond Negroid Africa to an area of Caucasoid dominance—which in turn leads us to North Africa and to the Near East itself.

The pan-Islamic tradition

We have already noted the southern migration of Moslem culture along the East coast of Africa; through our Philippine and Indonesian discussions, we have intimated something of its eastward expansion out of the Near East into Central and Southern Asia. We turn now to the mainstream of Western Islamic culture. This can be found in a roughly crescent-shaped expanse of territory extending from Spain along the African Coast of the Mediterranean and up through the Near East where it splits in the direction of Iran and via Turkey into East Europe. At the terminals of this crescent the traditions are quite mixed, particularly in East Europe. However, within the non-European confines of the crescent —that is, from Morocco to Turkey—there is a unity of culture which I shall label the *pan-Islamic tradition*, realizing that historically and geographically the areas placed under this category include such non-Islamic groups as Near Eastern Christians and Jews as well as pre-Islamic Arabs. This label encompasses a variety of peoples such as the Turks of Central Asian origin, the Aryan Persians, many kinds of Arab and Semitic peoples, and the Hamitic converts of North Africa. One can expect many differences within such a large grouping of peoples, but the pan-Islamic label is still useful, for the spread of Islam has directly or indirectly brought certain unifying elements to this vast area.

Our discussion of pan-Islamic music will fall into the three general categories of folk, art, and popular, recognizing that extensive interpenetration of styles and instruments has occurred between these three ill-defined genres. Under these three categories representative examples will be chosen from one or both of two sub-areas within the pan-Islamic crescent. One is the desert and the so-called Maghrib, the North African Coast including the modern nations of Morocco, Algeria, Tunisia, and Libya, with Egypt as a cultural buffer zone between this area and the next. The other section is the Near East proper, which includes Iran, Syria, Iraq, Jordan, Lebanon, Saudi Arabia, Oman, Aden, and Yemen. For most of this survey Turkey will be included in this latter area, though its Central Asian background gives it many special traits. Hebraic Palestine (Israel) will be treated separately.

Pan-Islamic folk music

The dominant pre-Islamic peoples of North Africa were the Berbers. With the seventh-century entrance of Islam and the eleventh-century migrations of Bedouin Arabs, the Berbers were pushed into the mountains or out onto the desert where they, in turn, displaced Negro groups. Today the Berbers are Moslem, but many times their present culture reveals a patchwork of Moslem and indigenous ideas. This can be seen in the life of the Tuaregs, the so-called "Abandoned of God," who control caravan routes in the Sahara Northeast of Timbuktu.

Unlike most Berbers, the Tuaregs adopted the Moslem social system while sharing Berber monogamy. Their form of matriarchy is unique (only the men wear veils), as is their writing system (only the women are literate). Their music shows similar contrasts. When women sing, ornaments characteristic of the Moslem music of this area are missing and the accompaniment is only percussion or handclapping, though a characteristic Arab female yodelling cry is often interjected. The two Tuareg percussion instruments are normally played only by women. One is the single-headed *tendi* kettle drum, played with the hands and tuned by dampening the gazelle-skin head. The other is the so-called water drum—actually an idiophone consisting of a large bowl of water in which a second bowl has been placed upsidedown. A stick is used to beat out a simple rhythm on the upturned bowl.

Photographs show men playing tambourines, but traditionally women are the instrumentalists. Men, however, do sing, particularly at the sensuous *ahal* entertainment gatherings. They perform highly ornamented love songs to the accompaniment of a one-stringed spike fiddle (*amzhad* or *imzhad*—Plate IV, figure 12), often played by the female object of their song. The heterophonic nature of these songs can be seen in the excerpt shown in Example 3-1.

From this discussion it seems that Tuareg women's music is more oriented toward some non-Moslem style, possibly derived from old Berber culture or from the music of their Negro slaves; on the other hand, male music seems Moslem. During the holy Ramadan month the Tuaregs sometimes join with Arabs and Moslem Negros at an oasis for a night of ecstatic dancing. The uinque musical mixtures of this trance-filled night offer dramatic illustration of the continuous interchange of ideas in the desert.

Along the coast and in the mountains of North Africa the pan-Islamic

EXAMPLE 3-1. A heterophonic Tuareg love song transcribed from the recording, *Tuareg Music of the Southern Sahara* (New York: Folkways Record FE 4470), side 1, band 3. By permission of Folkways Records and Service Corporation.

style prevails. There are, however, occasional remnants of the Greco-Roman occupation of the land as well as specific Berber or Jewish songs. The expulsion of the Sephardic Jews and later the Moors from Spain in the fifteenth century had its musical effect on North Africa as well. Earlier, during the heydays of Moorish Spain, the various courts in Morocco, Tunisia, and Algeria learned much about Arab classical music from Hispanic artists. The thirteenth-century Bedouin invasion destroyed this

Berber culture and its economy, so that today Berber songs and dances are best found only in the remote Atlas mountains of Algeria. However, even these remnants exhibit traits common to the entire pan-Islamic tradition. For example, a description of Berber mountain dances notes the typical Arab circling line-dance pattern and the use of tambourine accompaniment.[3]

If one goes north of the mountains and out onto the coastal plains, the Islamic influence becomes even clearer. Professional epic poets appear, and they are often accompanied by an end-blown flute commonly called the *gasba* or *qasaba*. The Near Eastern equivalent of this is called the *nay*. Both instruments have five or six finger holes and tend to be played slanted slightly to the side of the player in a manner reminiscent of both the *sib* of ancient Egypt and the *suling* of modern Indonesia. *Gasba* are made of either cane or metal. Whether such flutes play heterophonic vocal accompaniments or free·rhythmic solos, their florid, breathy melodies are typically pan-Islamic.

A majority of pan-Islamic folk music is purely vocal. It is either performed as a solo or in call and response with a unison chorus as shown in Example 3-2. If accompaniment is desired, the most common type is a handclap on the main accent of a duple meter (Example 3-2). The most popular instrumental addition is the tambourine. It comes in several distinct forms throughout the pan-Islamic world and is called by a dozen names, the most common of which are *duff*, *taar*, and *bendair*. Its basic form is a circular, single-headed frame drum, either plain or with snares attached beneath the skin. Metal disks may be set in the frame or metal rings attached around the inside of the rim behind the skin. There are also diamond- and square-shaped tambourines. Regardless of its shape or size, the tambourine is a vital element in most lively forms of pan-Islamic music —particularly dances, wedding songs, and other music sung primarily by women.

Wedding songs are a significant part of pan-Islamic female music. These are often performed by professional singers hired for the occasion. Weddings also require another typical pan-Islamic instrument, the double-reed aerophone known in the Maghrib as the *zukra*, *zamr*, or *gaita* (Plate VI, figure 18). It is more commonly known in the Near East by the Persian term *surnay* or the Turkish *zurna* (*zorna*). This double-reed, conical aerophone normally has seven holes on top and one in the back. The standard Western imitations of Near Eastern music are inspired by its nasal, "outdoor" sound. Most players place the reed inside the mouth so that no lip pressure is possible. When the instrument is played in this way, the bulging cheeks of the player are, in fact, the bag of a human bagpipe. Actual bagpipes with and without drones are found throughout the

---

[3] See Alexis Chottin, *Tableau de la musique marocaine* (Paris: Geuthner, 1939), Chapter 1.

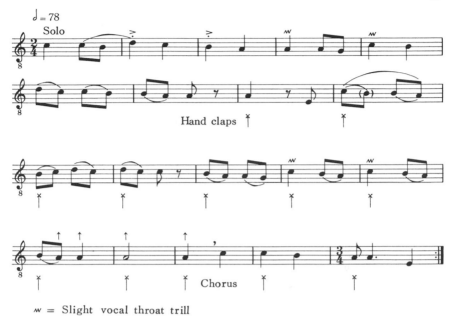

ᴡ = Slight vocal throat trill

EXAMPLE 3-2. A Druse song transcribed from the recording *Arabic and Druse Music* (New York: Folkways Record P 480), side 1, band 6. By permission of Folkways Records and Service Corporation.

Maghrib as well as up the Nile River in the Sudan. However, a more common pan-Islamic aerophone is the double clarinet shown in figure 13 of Plate IV. Standard names for it are the *argul, yarul, zamr,* or *zamar.* It is sometimes mislabelled as a double flute or double reed. Properly described, it is a double clarinet, for it consists of two cylindrical pipes each of which has a single free reed. These are placed inside the mouth and vibrate freely. Sometimes the reeds are within a wooden cup which the player places against his face, thus avoiding the need to "swallow" the reeds. One may play parallel melodies on the two pipes or use one as a drone. Since there are normally five or six finger holes on each pipe and only four fingers available on each hand for playing, one might wonder about the function of the extra holes. They may be plugged to change the pitch level of the melody or drone (note the bottom hole of the right-hand pipe in figure 13). Since there are no octave holes in the rear of the pipes, *argul* melodies are restricted to a six- or seven-note range. However, by using nasal breathing a good player can keep up a lively stream of music so that the tone never stops. This instrument comes in all sizes; the largest is found in Egypt, where the drone pipe is some four feet long.

There are three characteristic membranophones of the pan-Islamic world besides the tambourine. The word *tabl* or some variant of it is used

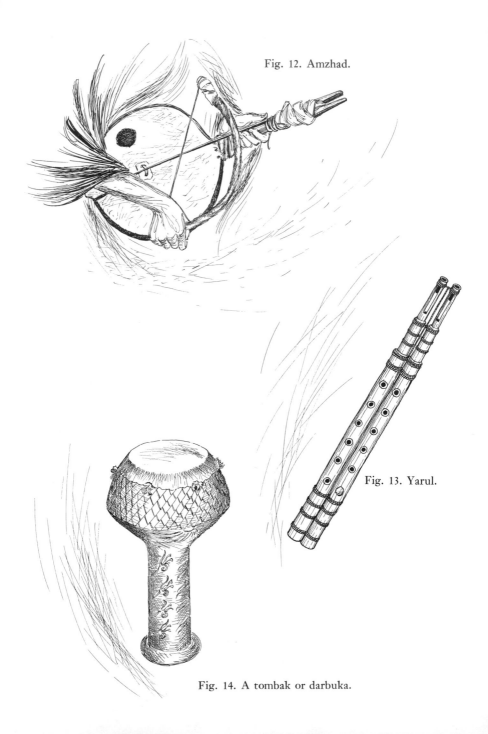

PLATE IV. *The Near East*

Fig. 12. Amzhad.

Fig. 13. Yarul.

Fig. 14. A tombak or darbuka.

to designate most cylindrical drums as well as several with kettle-shaped bodies. An inseparable pair of small kettle drums called *naqqara* is found even as far east as Tibet. Indeed, it may be that some instruments such as these *naqqara* came from Central Asia to the Near East with the migrations of the various Turkic peoples. Today this instrument is likely to show up in the cafe orchestras rather than in folk music. The same may be said for the most popular pan-Islamic drum of all, the single-headed drum, with a pottery or metal vase body, called the *darbuka, darabukka,* or *tombak* (shown in figure 14 of Plate IV). It can be played in any one of three ways: upright, tucked under the left arm, or held upside down and struck from below. In any position it provides a very lively beat for Arab music of all kinds.

Stringed instruments do not play a significant role in North African folk music except for the bowed spike fiddle of the street musicians and the plucked lyre of the Sudan and Northeast Africa. The Moroccan Berber, however, do have a three-stringed plucked lute called the *lutar,* and throughout North Africa one can find many homemade versions of the two-stringed *genibri* or *gunbri.* This indigenous plucked lute has a rectangular, skin-covered body and a round neck.

In Turkey and parts of the Near East, several different plucked and bowed lutes can be found in folk ensembles. Figure 16 of Plate V shows a *tambur,* a popular Near Eastern plucked lute. It has a small, pear-shaped wooden body, a long fretted neck, and from two to ten metal strings in double courses. A common variant is the *buzuq,* usually with three double courses (six strings). The most widespread folk forms in Turkey and Turkish-influenced East Europe are the nine-stringed *saz,* the six-stringed *baglama,* and the eight-stringed *bozuq.* The *kemanche,* used throughout Turkey and Persia, is a bowed lute with three or four strings that finds its way into Europe through the many *lira* and other bowed lutes of East Europe and Greece. It is also one of the important ancestors of the European *rebec,* which eventually evolved into the Western violin. This cycle was completed in recent centuries when the Western violin was, in turn, used by Moslem musicians as a substitute for the *rebab,* from which it originated.

So far we have noted wedding songs, love songs, epic tales, and line dances (the *dabka* or *debka*) as typical pan-Islamic folk forms. To these we must add various religious songs in praise of the saints or in honor of pilgrims returning from Mecca, as well as the special songs of splinter Moslem sects and the ecstatic chants of the dervish groups. Liturgical music as such is very restricted in orthodox Mohammedanism, since the prophet had a decided anti-musical bias.[4] The calls to prayer (*adhan* or *azan*) by the muezzin from the minaret are usually quite ornate while the

---

[4] A collection of English translations of the major religious comments against music is found in M. L. Choudhury, "Music in Islam," *The Journal of the Asiatic Society, Letters* (1957) XXIII, No. 2.

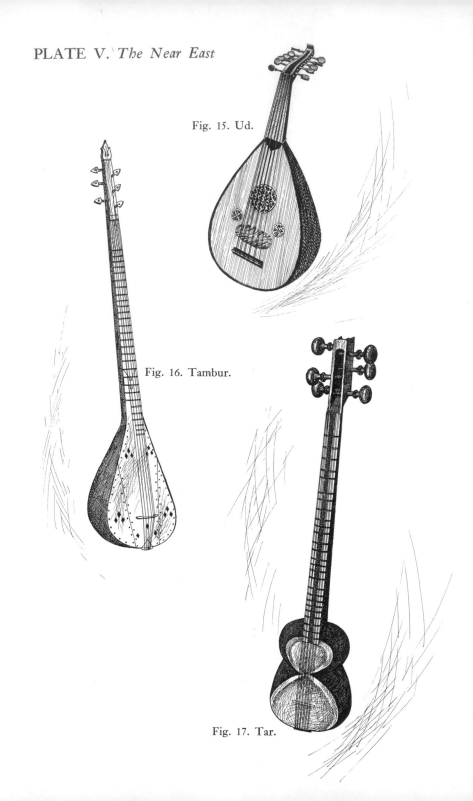

PLATE V. *The Near East*

Fig. 15. Ud.

Fig. 16. Tambur.

Fig. 17. Tar.

intoning of prayers and sections from the Koran in the mosque is done to specific, restrained chants. Both the call to prayers and such chants, in fact, are not considered to be music and therefore are acceptable within the mosque. Another example of such "nonmusic music" in the pan-Islamic world is the recitation of certain classical poetry. Both examples are useful reminders of the fact that different cultures have different definitions of the word music.

Pan-Islamic ceremonial music outside the mosque is best heard at weddings, funerals, and other special family events. Such occasions usually require the service of the wailing *zurnas* and various drums. During the Ramadan holy month in North Africa these oboes and even horns (*neffar* or *nafir*) are used for the call to prayers. In addition, one may hear wandering bards playing one-stringed fiddles and singing *qasida*, songs praising the careers of Mohammed (A.D. 570-632) and the saints. Today these itinerant *qasida* tend to deal with more current events, though they may retain an opening line in praise of their God. The term *qasida*, however, is better known as part of the classical music that is heard today in the cafes and in private concerts.

Pan-Islamic classical music theory

As intimated earlier, there were many centers of musical culture throughout the Islamic world. The oldest was probably pre-Islamic Persia, which itself contained remnants of ancient Babylonian thought as well as some infusions of Greek ideas. This area was conquered by the Arabs in the seventh century. Its musical traditions were then mixed with those of the Arabs. As sultanates proliferated along the ever-extending line of Islamic conquests, Moslem musicians and music theorists found patronage in courts as far distant as Samarkand in Central Asia and Salamanca in Spain.

The defeat of Islam in Spain in 1492 forced the Iberian scholars to flee to North Africa, so that today there is a school of so-called Andalusian classical music in the Maghrib. The rise of the Ottoman Turkish empire from the thirteenth through the sixteenth centuries maintained other centers of activity, such as Alexandria and Bagdad. Though this last great Moslem empire was politically rather static until its demise in the twentieth century, its musicians remained creative and active through at least the eighteenth century.

The historical outline given above is reflected in the contemporary scene, for the modern Moslem classical music tradition can be divided into four major schools: the Persian, with its center in Iran; the Arab, which flourishes strongly in Egypt; the Andalusian, as it is practiced in North Africa; and the Turkish. Modern practitioners from the various national schools that lie within these four larger traditions continue to expand the theory and practice of their art, but they all retain certain basic concepts that we can label as the pan-Islamic classical music theory.

The apogee of Moslem music theory came in the ninth and tenth centuries, when scholars such as Al Kindi (*d.c.* 870) and Al Farabi (*d.* 950) combined Greek, Persian, and Arab concepts into a brilliant synthesis. Al Farabi's "Grand Book of Music" (*Kitab al musiqi al kabin*) is one of the monuments of music theory and was read at the medieval University of Paris as well as in Salamanca and Bagdad. One of the first considerations of such books was the formation of scales, so we shall turn to that topic next (although our view will concentrate on the work of modern Moslem scholars rather than of the ancients).

Pan-Islamic music is conceived within the framework of a system called *maqamat* (plural of *maqam*) which determines the modal as well as the melodic basis upon which musical compositions are formed. The scales of the *maqamat* are divisive, that is, the notes are based on the principle of deriving different tones from the various divisions of a vibrating string. Originally, the resulting proportions of these string lengths were permutated mathematically to create several different divisions to the octave. Using the fretted fingerboard of a lute (the *ud*, Plate V, figure 15) as a diagram, a great number of modes was constructed, based on the vocabulary of these divisions. These "finger modes" were arranged in various geometrical figures—such as circles, stars, and polygons—designed to show the link of each mode with specific moods, times of the day, seasons, colors, and other extra-musical concepts.

Over the centuries the number of divisions of the Moslem octave changed many times (25, 17, 15, etc.), as did the names and construction of the various scales. Thus there is little consistency today in the use of scale names. This can be seen in Example 3-3, which shows three North African scales, all called *ramal maia* coming from three adjacent countries. The Algerian example is called *o'shak* (*'ushshaq*) by the East Arabs.

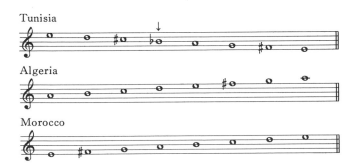

EXAMPLE 3-3. Three versions of the mode *ramal mai* from Alexis Chottin, *Tableau de la musique marocaine* (Paris: Geuthner, 1939), p. 181. Used by permission.

An Egyptian survey of Moslem music in 1932 showed that the Egyptians had 52 basic scales; the Syrians had the same number, some in altered form; North Africa had 18, 16 of them the Egyptians' scales under different names; Iraq had 37, 15 of them the Egyptian scales under different names; and the Iranians had 7, which they claimed could be permutated into all the others. In the midst of such variety and musical chauvinism, we shall discuss primarily the modern Iranian (or Persian) system as it is derived from the classical tradition. It can illustrate succinctly the general pan-Islamic approach to the basic theoretical problem of scale-formation.

Persian theory today has seven modal structures (*dastgah* or *dastgar*) and five related scales (*avaz*). These terms, like the Arab word *maqam*, imply cadence formulas and other melodic and aesthetic characteristics beyond those of a mere scale. Thus, when they are written out as scales there seem to be only 9 *dastgah*, but when they are played, the full 12 emerge. This is an important point, because any notation of pan-Islamic scales (see Examples 3-3 and 3-4) is not really a true representation of the *maqam* or *dastgah*. Most practicing Moslem musicians, in fact, are not concerned with scales as such. They play pieces rather than scales.

The basic Persian *dastgah* are shown in Example 3-4. On a fretted Persian instrument such as the *tar* (Plate V, figure 17) there are 15 intervals provided within the octave from which seven note scales are derived. Three of these 15 divisions are never played consecutively, so that the music is not actually microtonally chromatic, as some writings indicate. Rather, these divisions are combined into 4 different kinds of seconds (represented by letters in Example 3-4): a minor second (slightly less than 100 cents, m); the major second (approximately 200 cents, M); a neutral second (about 150 cents, N); and an enlarged second (some 255 cents, P). In addition, there is sometimes a neutral third of around 355 cents. The Persian scales may also use different intervals ascending and descending. (We must remember that we are dealing here with music theory and that in practice the various intervals listed above may vary considerably; nevertheless, their theoretical existence does exert a strong influence on the actual music, and many of these "out-of-tune" intervals are very accurately and artfully played by the virtuosi of Iran.)

While classical Persian music tends to be free in rhythm, Persian theory includes a concept of rhythmic modes or patterns (*darb*). This concept in the Arab world is known as *iqa'at*, in Egypt as *durub*, in Turkey as *usul*, and in the Maghrib as *mazim*. Each country has a varying number of these patterns. Arab theory, for example, claims up to 92 rhythmic patterns which come in many lengths from a few beats up to as many as 50. In Persia, there are some 30 named rhythmic patterns; they are usually no longer than 16 beats. Pan-Islamic rhythmic patterns in general are written out in relation to the tambourine or drum mnemonics by which they are learned. Such mnemonics appear below the Turkish version of the rhythmic pattern *remel* in Example 3-5. Two positions on the

EXAMPLE 3-4. The basic Persian *dastgah* from Hormoz Farhat, "Persian Classical Music," in *Festival of Oriental Music and the Related Arts* (Los Angeles: University of California Extension, 1960), 76. Used by permission.

staff have been used to help the reader visualize the different sounds on the instrument, without intending to suggest absolute pitch. Example 3-5 also includes the modern Arab version of the same-named pattern, to show that the major Islamic traditions need not always apply the same terms in vastly different ways (as was shown, for example, in Example 3-3).

These few comments on pan-Islamic theory have completely left out

EXAMPLE 3-5. Two versions of the rhythmic pattern *remel* derived from *Ency-clopédie de la musique*, A. Lavignac and L. de la Laurencie, eds. (Paris: Librairie Delagrave, 1922), pp. 2773 and 3054. Used by permission.

the extensive Moslem studies of the physics of sound and tuning. Further research would reveal in Islamic theory a subtle combination of mathematics, aesthetics, and philosophy. However, the real beauty of the system lies in the living art of musical performance.

Pan-Islamic classical music—performance practice

Modern Islamic classical music shows two general tendencies that have sometimes been labeled as the oriental and occidental sides of the Moslem tradition. The "oriental" style emphasizes improvisatory solos, but the "occidental" prefers the use of unison orchestras and choruses performing accurate reproductions of florid but not freely ornamented traditional melodies. Both styles may appear within a given national tradition, depending on emphasis. However, we will begin our discussion with one of the most improvisatory forms, the *gushe* of Persian music.

The Iranian or Persian *gushe* has been described as a skeletal melody relating to a given mood. At present there are some two hundred and fifty *gushe*, each related to one or more of the basic modal structures (*dastgah*) discussed earlier. These are preserved in a collection known as the *radif*. However, this is a musical reference book rather than a collection of classical compositions in the Western sense of a set of famous piano sonatas, for example. The aim of the performer is to weave a gentle filigree of improvisation around the melodies listed in the *radif* in such a way that the basic characteristics of the melodic frame and the mode upon which each is based will emerge. This is usually done in a free rhythm so that the player may have ample time to pursue his musical imagination.

Gushe are commonly played on the end-blown *nay* flute or the two- to four-stringed Iranian *kamanja* (*kemanche*) spiked fiddle. The rather long spike of this bowed lute is attached to a globular or cylindrical body, which is faced with a thin membrane. It is the progenitor of a variety of similar Near Eastern instruments, many falling under the general term *kamanja*. Another lovely classical Persian instrument is the plucked, long-necked *tar* lute (Plate V, figure 17). It has six double courses of metal strings stretched over a membrane-faced figure eight shaped body. The gut frets along its neck are movable so that the player may adjust them to the requirements of a given mode. The term *tar* in the Near East and Central Asia is used as the final syllable in the names of many other plucked lutes. In Iran itself, for example, another common instrument is the four stringed *setar*. It resembles the *tambur* shown in figure 16. The terms *tambur* (often spelled *tanbur*) and *setar* will be shown to appear among a variety of other instruments when we move eastward out of Iran and Turkey in the next chapter.

The Persian dulcimer called the *santur* or *santir* is of special interest because it is the ancestor of a variety of instruments, from the Western cimbalom and piano to the Chinese *yang ch'in*. Seventy-two metal strings, in quadruple courses, are stretched over a shallow trapezoidal body and hit with two delicate hammers. Since the *santur* has no dampening devices, the florid sounds of a *gushe* played upon it tend to merge into an exotic mesh of tone color. Arab *santur* normally have 36 strings, and one Turkish model had 105. The stringing method for the *santur* varies from an alternate arrangement of pegs to having all the pegs on one side (as on the instrument in figure 19).

In addition to these many instrumental media for classical music there is the voice. We have already mentioned the importance of classical poetry recitation as a lyrical form of "nonmusic." Poetry can also be declaimed within a musical performance. In Iran, such performances include vocal realizations of a *gushe*. Many times, these are done in collaboration with an instrumentalist. In such cases, the player must listen to the singer's improvisation and elaborate on it, even as the singer is finishing, as shown in Example 3-6. All this, being done in a free rhythm, creates a kind of counterpoint that defies vertical codification. The art of the *gushe* is truly analogous to the delicate traceries carved around the entrance of a mosque or to the arabesques of Persian poetry.

EXAMPLE 3-6. A Persian *gushe* transcribed from the recording, *Iran* (Kassel: Bärenreiter-Musicaphon Record BM 30 L 2004), side 1, band 2. Used by permission.

If one moves out of Persia, there are still many sung poems and instrumental solos to be heard. Bowed lutes and flutes have already been shown to be popular solo instruments in North Africa. One of the most popular solo instruments, however, is the *ud*, shown in figure 15 of Plate V. It is a pear-shaped, plucked lute with a wooden soundboard and from eight to twelve gut strings, some of them in double courses. The fingerboard may or may not have gut frets. Many North African *uds* have ten strings but the Turkish *ude* has eleven, with five double courses and a single bass string.

The *ud* and its narrower-bodied, longer-necked variant, the *kwitra* (in Turkey the *lauta*), are also important instruments in the pan-Islamic orchestral tradition. Since these orchestras play in unison or in mild heterophony, they may consist of any number of different instruments. Their basic percussion instrument is some variety of tambourine, to which may be added the pot drum (*darbuka*) or, in Turkish-influenced orchestras, the small double kettle drums (*naqqara*). The end-blown flute and one of the plucked lutes mentioned above are normally present, as is some form of bowed lute. In North Africa this is often a four-stringed version of the violin called the *kamanja*, played upright on the knee with a rather straight bow; the Turks and East Arabs call this instrument the *keman*. In Morocco there may also be a special two-stringed form of the *rabab*. It has a fingerboard (unlike the variants shown in figures 8 and 12) that is actually a hollow extension of the body along its short neck to the peg box. The *santur* dulcimer also appears in many orchestras. Turkish-influenced ensembles may replace it with a *kanun* or *qanun* (Plate VI, figure 19), a zither with 72 strings plucked by small picks attached to the index fingers. Some Arab models have small levers under the strings at the peg side that make it possible to change the pitch slightly for different scale tunings. Whatever the combination of instruments may be, the basic function of these orchestras in classical music is to perform suites.

There are several kinds of Moslem suites, from the "occidental-style" Moorish- (that is, Spanish) based *nuba* or *nawba* of North Africa to the more "oriental" suites of Egypt and the Near East. All these suites consist of a series of instrument solos and orchestral selections interspersed with unison choral songs or solo recitatives based on classical poetry. In Persian music a group of *gushe* can also be performed in a suite-like manner. In the suites of North Africa and Egypt, all the principal sections are in the same *maqam*. Since there may be some eight or ten sections within a suite, one will find modulations to other modes within one section, but, in theory, the music should return to the original mode at the end of each digression. Within each movement of a suite there are usually several subsections, which go under the general name of *khana* or *cana*. Both these sections and the movements themselves can be differentiated by changes of mood and by the particular rhythmic patterns they employ.

The specific movements played in a given performance of classical music may vary. In addition, individual movements may be played separately. For example, the introductory solo improvisations of Arab suites

PLATE VI. *The Near East*

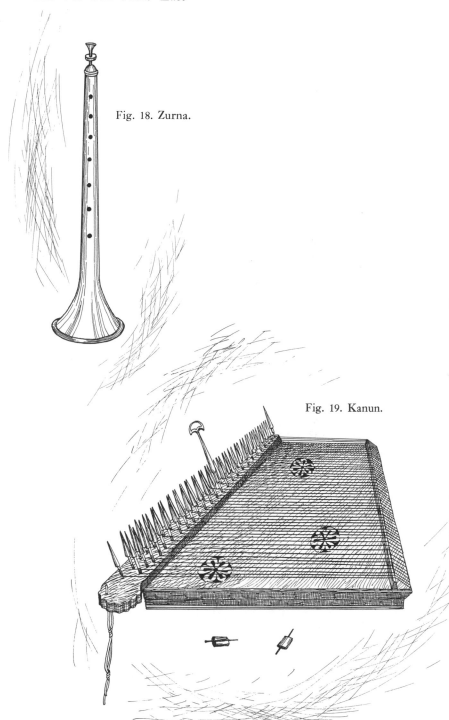

Fig. 18. Zurna.

Fig. 19. Kanun.

called *taqsim* are frequently heard in solo lute recitals. Their original intent was to set the basic mode, mood, and melodic phrases of the suite that would normally follow. Similarly, the Turkish-inspired *bashraf* or *peshrev* orchestral movements or the lighter-sounding *samai* make very acceptable concert pieces, since they have within them changes of tempo and mood. The singing of the *qasida* classical poems in Arab suites or in the sections called the *abyat* and the *barwal* in North African suites is also common. However, when pan-Islamic music is performed in its multi-movement form, it displays a subtlety of design and an architectonic structure that are the true intents of the Moslem artists. A sense of order is established in these suites through the early presentation of melodic and modal ideas that are then permutated throughout the various movements. At the same time, the set order of rhythmic changes gives to the knowledgeable listener a sense of logical progression in time as well as that feeling of anticipation so important to the active participation of any audience in a musical experience. This does not mean that a Moslem audience must necessarily listen with the kind of specific intellectual concentration that we attempt to instill into Western listeners through our music appreciation courses. Moslem classical music, rather like Moslem calligraphy, presents a large tracery of intersecting lines; one may choose to follow the peregrinations of a given melody or simply relax in the beauty of the general design. This attitude is reflected in the circumstances of performance of Moslem classical music, for, while there are some formal concerts in which the arrangement and deportment of the musicians and audience are strictly regulated (as they are in Western concert halls), this music is frequently heard in cafés. The listener may listen, sip, or converse as he sees fit. Here also, the classical tradition may be mixed with the new and the popular: A *taqsim* may be followed by a love song or by the music of that type of gyrating female dance for which the Near East is so famous. Classical ideals obviously suffer under such circumstances. However, the music of the modern café orchestras of the Near East and the Maghrib is an excellent example of the manner in which musical styles continue to interact throughout the world of music.

There is one more Moslem ensemble that must be mentioned, especially for its influence on Western music. It is the famous Turkish Janissary military band, which consisted of nine players each on bass drums (*dawul*), trombones (*boru*), cymbals, double kettle drums (*nakara*), *zurna* oboes, and the clanging bell trees called, in English, Turkish crescents or Chinese pavilions.[5] Many of the eighteenth-century pieces *alla turca* by such composers as Mozart and Beethoven were imitations of this ensemble. A modern variant of it can be heard in some Shriners' parades in the United States. However, most of the Moslem-sounding music heard in

---

[5] This group is pictured on page 125 of Reinhard Pauly's *Music in the Classic Period* (Englewood Cliffs, N.J.: Prentice-Hall, Inc., 1965).

the Euro-American world today is derived from the jauntier styles of pan-Islamic popular music.

Pan-Islamic popular music

There probably has been some kind of topical, easily learned entertainment music in every urbanized culture of the world. Today, telecommunications have created an additional kind of pan-world popular music by making the latest hits of Europe and America instantaneously available throughout the globe. However, the Near East, like the rest of the non-Western world, is not merely a passive receiver of this idiom. In addition to faithful reproductions of Western idioms it has produced its own form of synthesis from a mixture of Western and indigenous elements. Such compromises tend to follow typical lines.

First, Western tempered tuning takes over, and those native instruments incapable of performing in that tuning tend to drop out, often to be replaced by some similar Western instruments. The clarinet, for example, is often substituted for the *zurna* oboe. The vocal part becomes less florid and less nasal, and the melodies themselves tend to be phrased in the four-square manner of Western popular music and to use the reverting rather than the progressive form. If a lead singer is backed by a vocal group, as is common in many Western popular recordings, the group will sing a unison response, an ostinato, or occasionally a drone rather than harmony. Harmony may appear in pan-Islamic popular tunes through the use of a piano or accordion, though sometimes even these instruments will be played in a monophonic manner. One of the most revealing ways to discover the cavalier approach to harmony exhibited in many Arab popular tunes is to follow the bass part. It usually is more concerned with reproducing a standard Near Eastern rhythmic pattern than it is in creating a solid harmonic bass progression. However, sometimes this native rhythm pattern will be altered to fit into one of the standard South American dance forms such as the beguine, tango, or rumba. We said earlier that music styles do not remain static; pan-Islamic popular music is certainly a case in point.

A historical interlude—The Ancient World of the Near East

Although this book deals primarily with the contemporary scene, one cannot ignore the many evidences of music that come from the very cradle of civilization and give us our earliest clues as to the first uses of music by urbanized man.

The oldest records of the ancient civilizations show that music was already a highly organized activity. In Mesopotamia, for example, the presence of guilds of musicians can be traced back as early as the fourth millennium B.C. Among the endless legal documents that dominate the famous cuneiform clay tablet collections one can find contracts for singers from such guilds, employed to intone the psalms in Sumerian temples. Collections of Babylonian liturgies themselves indicate that large numbers of such singers were used, sometimes accompanied by reed pipes, flutes, drums, or tambourines. The excavations of Ur (twenty-fifth century B.C.) have actually revealed examples of such instruments as double pipes, clappers, and sistrums, along with an eleven-stringed harp that seems to be the progenitor of harps all along the ancient trade routes of the Orient to the far reaches of China and Japan.

Large ensembles of double pipes, percussion instruments, and various styles of harps are seen in the bas-reliefs of later Assyrian and Babylonian ruins. At the same time, written records show us that the ancients knew much about the science of music and acoustics and had evolved a complex theory of the relationship between music and other elements in the universe.

In Egypt, the earliest dynastic records also show a highly evolved art of music. Egyptian art from the twenty-sixth century B.C. shows male musicians playing various harps, reed pipes, and long, end-blown flutes. We noted earlier that the flutes (*sibs*) are held to the side as are most *nay* in the Near East today.

Continual change in musical taste was as true in the ancient world as it is today. In the New Kingdom (*circa* 1507 B.C.) foreign female musicians from the Near East became the favorites of the courts, and with them must have come new, "exotic" music. The walls of many tombs and monuments chronicle in much detail the eras of change in Egyptian music history. Yet the musicians who accompany the solemn rites and joyful dances pictured there are mute; no music remains. Like most Near Easterners today, the ancients seem to have taught their music by rote, and the sound apparently died with the performers. There have been attempts to decipher what may be a rudimentary notation involving hand gestures (chironomy) as seen in several wall paintings. In addition, studies of string lengths, frets, and finger holes in both pictures and artifacts have been used as the basis for inferences about Egyptian scales, and finger positions of harpists in drawings have been used to show the possible existence of harmonies in fourths or fifths.

There has been little agreement on the interpretation of these remnants, or regarding the one supposed example of music notation in cuneiform. This does not mean, however, that the musical legacy of the ancient world is completely lost. The Babylonian connection of music with the universe passed on into the Persian tradition. The Egyptians of Plato's time were still possessors of coveted knowledge in both music practice and theory. Thus, much that we credit to Pythagoras and other great Greek music theorists may have deeper roots in Alexandria and the Nile Valley. In addition, the legacy of ancient Egypt is found in the shapes, tunings, and playing styles of such folk instruments as the *argul* double clarinets in Egypt, the *genibri* of North Africa, the many end-blown flutes of the Near East, the *halam* of the Wolofs, and the sistrums of the Ethiopian Copts or the ancient Greeks and Romans.[6]

One of the most famous Egyptian harp songs was a funeral piece that said, "Let music and song be before you. Leave behind all evil and think only of joy until the day comes when we journey to that land that loves silence."[7] This seems a fitting tribute to the vitality that was, and the silence that now is, the condition of music from the ancient world.

Jewish music in the Near East

Among the several non-Moslem religious groups in the Near East, the Jews are the most numerous and widespread. Their tradition differs from the Moslem world in two ways. First, while the Moslem religion spread by conversion and conquest, the Jewish tradition remained basically esoteric and nonevangelistic. Wandering Jewish groups spread about the world but remained religiously separated from their host cultures. There was a cross-influence between Jewish and Gentile music cultures, particularly in the secular songs, but much of Jewish religious music held to older forms.

The second differences between the Jewish and Moslem worlds came with the creation of the state of Israel in 1948. Instead of a continual extension of cultural influence as in Islam, there was in Israel a sudden compression of co-religionists from widely scattered ethnic groups. This concentration of cultures has made Israel (and, for the same reason, cities like New York) a rich hunting ground for ethnomusicologists.

Each Jewish community in Israel today offers special musicological opportunities. The Yemenite Jews, for example, have been extensively studied in the belief that their music represents the oldest Near Eastern Jewish style. The Yemenite religious chant shown in Example 3-7 illustrates their tone-centered, ornamented litany style. The Sephardic Jews, by contrast, are studied for the *romanzas* of Spain that they have preserved since the time of their expulsion (1492). All the ghettos of Europe, the Jewish communities of Russia and the Near East, and even congrega-

---

[6] For a discussion of the survival of ancient Egyptian instruments see Hans Hickmann, *Catalogue d'enregistrements de musique folklorique égyptienne* (Strasbourg: Heitz, 1958).

[7] See Miriam Lichtheim, "The Songs of the Harpers," in *Journal of Near Eastern Studies*, IV, No. 1 (Jan., 1945), 178. My thanks go to Professor Carlton Hodge of Indiana University for advice on the paraphrase of the original translation.

EXAMPLE 3-7. A Yemenite Jewish chant transcribed from the recording, *Folk Music of Palestine* (New York: Folkways Record FE 4408), side 2, band 3. By permission of Folkways Records and Service Corporation.

tions from India have brought their unique musics to Israel. Once settled there, each group of such people tends to use four or five musical styles interchangeably.

First, there is the fairly unified liturgical style. After the destruction of the second temple (70 A.D.) by the Romans, the Jewish liturgy turned from sacrificial rites to an emphasis on prayers and invocations.[8] These have been passed on to every congregation. Thus, even distant groups seem to share the melismatic, free-rhythm cantillations of the cantor. Most Jewish cantillations are influenced by the dominant Near Eastern style and may even use modes related to *maqamat*. This is quite evident in the more ecstatic chassidic and cabalistic sects.

A second style is found in the singing of religious poems (*piyutim*). These show greater variety with many borrowings from Gentile traditions. The Jews, like the Protestant Christians, have used many secular tunes for such religious purposes. These tunes, in turn, have introduced new melodic styles into the Jewish tradition. For the Near Eastern Jew, the Moslem and Armenian-Russian folk songs were a great source. In Europe, each country has made its contributions to such music. The songs without words (*nigun*) of the chassidic sects are excellent examples of this kind of Jewish music.

A third tradition consists of the secular songs of the Israeli Jew's former homeland. Whether these songs are direct borrowings from a Gentile tradition or specific tunes from a ghetto, they reflect most clearly the land of their origin. Thus, one can hear the difference between a German Jew singing a thoroughly Teutonic piece or a Yiddish tune and the old homeland songs of a Rumanian or French Jew.

An Israeli Jew may pick up as a fourth tradition the pan-Islamic style that exists all·around him. When he does so he will completely change his vocal style and idiom. Such changes in style are not uniquely Jewish. For example, every American Christian youth uses a voice quality on Saturday

[8] The Negro Falasha Jews of Ethiopia still maintain the sacrificial rites, but they are a group quite apart from the Hebrew congregation.

night totally different from the one he uses on Sunday morning. This fact, unfortunately, cannot be shown in present-day music notation. Nevertheless, such things as voice quality, facial expression, and gesture should be included in the ideal description of a musical style.[9]

The fifth tradition of the Israelite Jew is the music of the modern state. The bond of Israel is religious or political, not ethnic. Therefore, there has been a concentrated effort on the part of Zionist musicians to "create" a new secular folk music. This music is actually a kind of popular music composed by professional songsmiths and deriving its inspiration from the agricultural, economical, and political aspirations of the state and its citizens. The instruments used to accompany such music reflect the acculturation of styles that is Israel. Near Eastern tambourines and vase drums may be combined with a short block flute (*halill*) and European guitars and accordions, sometimes as an accompaniment for the *hora*, a Near Eastern line dance. The modes of the melodies are often Near Eastern, but they are harmonized with European or Russian chords that discourage the use of indigenous nontempered notes.

The harmonic tendencies of secular music have come into the synagogues, as well, where choirs sing harmony while electric organs play irrelevant chords behind the cantor's melos. As we said before, the study of any music culture presents only moments in a time continuum, not finalities. The unusual polyethnic quality of Israel has created a striking musical mixture.

Bibliography and discography

Norma McLeod's "The Status of Musical Specialists in Madagascar," *Ethnomusicology*, VIII, No. 3 (Sept., 1964) shows the anthropological approach to music studies while Curt Sachs's *Les Instruments de musique de Madagascar* (Paris: Institut d'Ethnologie, 1938) is organological. Hugh Tracey's *Chopi Musicians* (London: Oxford University Press, 1948) gives considerable cultural and poetical detail on xylophone orchestra music. The sound may be heard in the Folkways Album *Africa South of the Sahara* (FE 4503). Arab-influenced West African music is found on Folkways *Wolof Music of Senegal and Gambia* (FE 4462). Folkways *Tuareg Music of the Southern Sahara* (FE 4470) is nicely documented by Geoffrey Holiday, who also wrote "The Tuaregs of the Ahaggar" in *African Music*, 1, No. 3 (1956). Wolfgang Laade produced three excellent volumes of Tunisian folk, religious, and art music on Folkways *Tunisia* (FE 8861, 8862, 8863), and Wolf Lesau has annotated *Music of South Arabia* (FE 4421). *Music of the Falashas* (FE 4442), and *Music of Ethiopia* (FE 4405). Good notes accompany *Arabic and Druse Music* (FE 4480). Other related Folkways releases are *Coptic Music* (FR 8960), *Islamic Liturgy* (FR 8943), *Kurdish Folk Songs and Dances* (FE 4469), and popular

[9] Attempts have been made to include them in style description. See Alan Lomax, "Folk Song Style," *The American Anthropologist*, 61 (1959), 917-954.

music in *Arabic Songs of Lebanon and Egypt* (FW 6925). *Folk and Traditional Music of Turkey* (FE 4404) and *Songs and Dances of Turkey* (FW 8801) contain a mixture of styles. Musicaphon has produced three volumes of pan-Islamic classical music, *Tunisia* (BM 30 L 2008), and two of the Persian tradition in *Iran* (BM 30 L 2004 and 2005).

Baron Rodolphe D'Erlanger presents fine transcriptions of Hispanic-Arab, Berber, Jewish, and Negro music in *Mélodies tunisiennes* (First Series, Vol. 3, of the *Bibliothèque Musicale du Musée Guimet*, Paris: Geuthner, 1937). He also produced a six-volume collection of Arab theorists, *La Musique arabe* (Paris: Geuthner, 1930-49). One of Alexis Chottin's several excellent writings on North Africa is *Tableau de la musique marocaine* (Paris: Geuthner, 1939). The articles in *Grove's Dictionary of Music* (5th Edition, 1954) by Henry George Farmer on Berber, Moorish, Maghribi, Persian, Syrian, and Turkestani music are useful summaries. Farmer's orientation is usually historical, as in his *A History of Arabian Music* (London: Luzac, 1929). More about the living tradition is found in F. Salvador-Daniel, *Arab Music and Musical Instruments* (New York: Charles Scribner's Sons, 1915). Edith Gerson-Kiwi is Israel's best musicologist in both Jewish and Arab studies. She deals with actual musical problems as well as those of history in her *The Persian Doctrine of Dastgar Composition* (Tel Aviv: Israel Music Institute, 1963) and "Women's Songs from the Yemen," in *The Commonwealth of Music*, Reese & Brandel, eds. (New York: the Free Press of Glencoe, Inc., 1965). A. Z. Idelsohn's *Jewish Music* (New York: Holt, Rinehart & Winston, Inc., 1929) is a standard general reference. The two Westminster records *In Israel Today* (W 9805, 9806) show some of the variety of music found in Israel. Dozens of modern Israeli music records are available, particularly on Elektra and Vanguard labels. Hans Hickmann is the major scholar of ancient Egyptian music, as seen in his *45 Siècles de musique dans l'Egypte ancienne* (Paris: Richard-Masse, 1956). The bibliographies and articles dealing with the ancient Near East in Volume One of *The New Oxford History of Music* (London: Oxford University Press, 1957) are good starting places for further study as is Curt Sachs's *The Rise of Music in the Ancient World East and West* (New York: W. W. Norton & Company, Inc., 1943).

4

Central and Southern Asia

Music of the Soviet
Central Asian Republics

The territories east of Turkey and west of China are known today as the Soviet Southern and Asian Republics. They include the Southern Republics of Georgia, Armenia, and Azerbaijan on the west shore of the Caspian Sea; the Central Asian Republics of Kazakhstan and Turkmenistan on the eastern shore; and Uzbekistan, Tadjikstan, and Kirghizstan still farther to the east. For most Westerners this area is a *terra incognita*, but historically it has been a land of many civilizations and many visitors. Some of its travelers have been merely observers or merchants—like Marco Polo—but a majority of those who crossed the borders of Central Asia had more militaristic or evangelistic intentions. A list of these visitors includes the feared names of the leaders of every horde that poured out of Inner

Asia toward the plunder of Europe and the Near East, such as Jenghiz Khan, Kublai Khan, and Tamerlane; it also includes the eastward-moving standard-bearers of Islam as well as the westward-directed advance guards of ancient Chinese armies. In a word, this area, plus Afghanistan to the south, contained the major routes of commerce and conquest for centuries. The results were a series of colorful and generally short-lived cultures as varied as the outside influences that pressed in upon them.

Today, the major influences to be found in Soviet Asia are the Persian and the Arab. This is easily seen in the presence of such musical instruments as the end-blown flute (*nai*), the conical oboe (*zurna*), and various double clarinets. The tambourine (commonly called the *doira* here) and the small pair of kettle drums (*nagora*) are also present. All the chordophones of Persia can be found, particularly in the art music ensembles of Tadjikstan, Uzbekistan, and Azerbaijan. Such ensembles play suites in the best pan-Islamic tradition. In Tadjikstan and Uzbekistan these suites are known as *makom*, while the Azerbaijan suites are sometimes called *dastgya*. These two terms obviously relate to the Near Eastern words *maqam* and *dastgah*, though their meanings are changed. Many other terms, such as mode names and the titles of movements within the suites, relate to the pan-Islamic tradition discussed in the previous chapter, but their uses often reflect specific Central Asian national styles.

We have noted that several centers of Moslem music theory were located in Central Asia. Al Farabi himself is said to have been born in Turkmenistan, and the eleventh-century theorist Ibn Sina (known in the West as Avicenna) was educated in Bokhara. These men were but two of many scholars who contributed to the general progress of Moslem music theory. Of more importance to the Central Asian art-music tradition was the work of Kaukaba (*d.* 1526). He made a definitive analysis of the *Shashmakom*, the basic collection of *makom* suites upon which all modern Tadjik and Uzbek classical performances are based. Another important innovator was Njaz Mitzabashi Kamil (*d.* 1889), who created a tablature called *khorezm* notation, in which the entire *tambur* part of the *Shashmakom* was written.

If one moves from the art music of Central Asia to the folk and popular idioms, many variations upon Near Eastern instruments can be found. Variants on the small-bodied, long-necked plucked lute such as the *tambur* (Plate V, figure 16) or *setar* are found in the two-stringed *dutar*, the three-stringed *komuz*, and the two-stringed *dombra*. The last comes in a great variety of shapes, some of which are influenced by still further variants of the same chordophone (for example, the *balalaika*). Despite the interrelations of the instrumental types, the musics played upon these various forms are not necessarily the same. Example 4-1 is the beginning of a Kirghiz song with *komuz* accompaniment. Organal harmonic accompaniments in parallel fifths or fourths and heterometric structures like those illustrated are common throughout Central Asia and seem to be indigenous elements in this highly acculturated music. There is also a fondness in Central Asia for double clarinets or for oboes with drones. Note in Example 4-1 the Central Asian tendency to use a neutral third (a sharp A in our transcription).

EXAMPLE 4-1. A *komuz* song from Kirghizstan transcribed from the recording, *Folk Music of the U.S.S.R.* (New York: Folkways Record FE 4535), side 4, band 3. By permission of Folkways Records and Service Corporation.

Another important feature of Central Asian music is the presence of long epic narratives. It is from the traditionally unaccompanied songs of their storytellers that many of the famous folk epics of this area have been recovered. Competitive songs are also found in which the contestants vie with each other through improvised verses in a manner quite like that found throughout the Romance-language countries of Europe.

Modern Soviet Asian music has been subjected to considerable collectivization under the general communist policy of "reconstruction," in which folk art must, by Marxist definition, reflect the social and political conditions of the people. This policy produces several curious results. First, field collectors are instructed to collect only such music as falls within these ideological goals and to admonish singers who persist in performing overly religious, sarcastic, or sensual musics. Secondly, the analysis of such music as is collected is made to conform to certain specific state doctrines such as the predominance of the 12-note chromatic scale system in peoples' music. In Central Asia the latter policy is the cause of much scholarly hedging as more and more "wrong notes" show up in the Islamic ornamented styles. Finally, the goal of collecting is not solely the archival preservation of traditional materials (though much valuable work is done in this area); rather, the music collected is primarily raw material for the use of Western-style composers who must produce new realistic music[1] based on national idioms. The music is also frequently arranged for state-supported "folk" orchestras and choruses, which then become the major media through which the music is made available to the people in performances and records.

Many individual folk singers are honored by the state, particularly if they create new socialist-oriented songs. However, the emphasis is on ensemble and choral music. This reflects the basically collective nature of the Soviet attitude toward music. Since the original idiom is often soloistic, musical collectivization is bound to affect such characteristics as ornamentation and tuning. The specific arrangements of reconstructed music reflect a strong orientation toward such ideals of the central conservatory in Moscow as harmony and tempered scales. The net result of these policies is a scarcity of what Western scholars would call authentic recordings and transcriptions, but an abundance of nationalistic musical activity supposedly based on the generally unavailable source material. What has actually been created is a kind of state-controlled popular music that often contains most of the same characteristics we noted in the popular music of the modern Middle East (see page 57). It remains to be seen how well national idioms flourish under such conditions. At the moment, modern Central Asian music often sounds suspiciously like nineteenth-century Russian romanticism when it is subjected to Marxist reconstruction.

Afghanistan

The twentieth-century country of Afghanistan shares borders with China, India, Pakistan, Iran, and Asiatic Russia. In ancient times these borders, like those of the Central Asian republics just discussed, were crossed many times by the routes of commerce or conquest. One artistic result of this constant flow of cultures can be seen in the amazing statuary found in the ruins of Afghanistan's ancient cities. The physical features of these statues are those of every type within the Indo-Caucasian family plus a liberal sprinkling of Mongoloids. Thus Afghanistan is an important link in the chain of cultures binding Europe and Asia together.

[1] The specific doctrines of Marxist music can be read in Rena Moisenco, *Realist Music* (London: Meridian, 1949).

Musically, this linkage can be heard by listening to pieces from various regions of Afghanistan. The western and northern musics of the country are dominated by Near Eastern or Central Asian styles, while Eastern Afghan music is heavily Hindu-oriented. The former tend to use a slightly nasal, quickly ornamented vocal line while the latter prefers a softer, lower tone quality and artful portamento slides.

The musical instruments of Afghanistan clearly show an interlocking of cultures. The two-stringed, bowed *ritchak* lute is related to the Near Eastern *rabab* although, like its Central Asian counterpart, its body is often made of a rectangular gasoline can. The Afghan and Central Asian instrument called the *rabab*, by contrast, is a plucked lute. The Near Eastern *tambur* and *setar* become the three-stringed plucked *tumbur* in Afghanistan, and the nonmelodic *tambura* of India becomes the melodic *dambura*.

Finally, one finds, in addition to the Near Eastern tambourines and pot drums, the two-headed *dhol* barrel drum common to Central and Southern India. From this morass of floating and changing terms, one fact is clear: a musical journey from West to East in Afghanistan moves us out of a basically Islamic culture and into a whole new world of music. This world is best studied at its center, India.

India—A historical introduction

The Indian Peninsula from the Himalayan Mountains and Karakorum to the island of Ceylon includes a wide variety of peoples, languages, religions, and political divisions. The history of this wide area began with the Dravidian civilization (2500-1900 B.C.), which was in turn supplanted by an Aryan invasion. The caste system—a Dravidian legacy—and the Hindu religion were already ancient traditions when Gautama Buddha (563-483 B.C.) appeared. Though the Buddhist religion eventually found its greatest strength outside India, the island of Ceylon remained a Buddhist stronghold. On the mainland, Hinduism was the dominant force until the Moslem invasion of the thirteenth century. The resultant Moghul courts of North India produced brilliant new Islamic-Indian art forms, while South India became the center of Hindu tradition. The British occupation of the nineteenth and twentieth centuries introduced many Western ways, but the basic cultural patterns of India remained those of the Moslem-Hindu world. The political separation of Pakistan from India in the mid-twentieth century is a reflection of this split cultural heritage. The musical division of India follows a similar pattern, although not the same boundaries. The music of Pakistan and North India where the Moslem influence is often stronger is called *Hindustan music*, while the more purely Indian music of the South is called *Karnatic music*. The Karnatic system prevails in Madras, Mysore, Andhra, and Kerala. Hyderabad may be said to be the dividing line between the Hindustani and Karnatic systems. Though these two systems use different instruments and vary in nomenclature, their basic concepts are the same and have been cultivated in India for centuries.

Ancient Indian music

The study of Indian art music begins with the *Vedic hymns*, based on the ancient Upanishads literature. The oldest collection of these hymns, the *Rig Veda*, was consolidated by at least the second millennium B.C. and is perhaps the oldest continuous vocal tradition in the world. There is, of course, no way of telling how close contemporary performance practice is to the original, but there are several extra-musical factors that might contribute to the preservation of its ancient traditions. In India, the physical vibrations of musical sound (*nada*) have always been inextricably connected with the spiritual and metaphysical world. As a result, the intoned word has great power in its combination of religious text and musical sound. Thus, the correct singing of a vedic hymn is essential not only to the validity of the ritual but also to the stability of the universe. Under such conditions the preservation of style would be at a premium.

The style of Rig Veda hymns is basically syllabic, with close attention paid to word accent, as shown in Example 4-2. The later collection of

EXAMPLE 4-2. A Rig Veda hymn transcribed from the recording, *India* (Kassel: Bärenreiter-Musicaphon Record BM 30 L 2006), side 1, band 2. Used by permission.

Sama Veda hymns, though using many Rig Veda texts, is, by contrast, quite wide-ranged, melismatic, and generally unconcerned with word accent. Though today there are various schools of vedic singing, the two basic approaches to the performance of these two collections of hymns stand as supporting pillars for any entrance into the world of Indian art music. The keystone of this entranceway is not music but a book, the *Natya Sastra*.

The *Natya Sastra* is attributed to Bharata. It is commonly dated in the fifth century A.D., although some have dated it as early as the second century B.C., and others feel that it is a compilation of the works of many men done between the fifth and seventh centuries A.D. Whatever its date, it is the traditional link between ancient India and the classical eighteenth- and nineteenth-century traditions as they survive today. While the book deals primarily with drama, it also contains an important discussion of music theory. All the Indian musical studies that followed began with interpretation of the musical sections of the *Natya Sastra*. However, they were often based on totally different current musical traditions, so that the meanings of various terms have changed radically over the centuries. One of the most important restatements of Hindu theory is the thirteenth-century *Samgita Ratnakara* done by Sarunga Deva during the time of pressures of Near Eastern thought brought in by the Moghul rulers. From the sixteenth through the nineteenth centuries, Indian theorists continued to attempt further syntheses and standardizations so that today the ancient terms remain but their definitions refer either to what ancient music *might* have been or to how these terms could be used to describe later musical practices. Nevertheless, the basic concepts and terminologies of the Vedic hymns, the *Natya Sastra*, and the *Samgita Ratnakara* are necessary for any beginning steps in the understanding of Indian music.

Indian music theory

Since word meanings in Indian music have changed so greatly over the centuries, it is obvious that we can deal here only with the more commonly accepted uses of musical terms and that we must leave their subtler and older meanings to the writings of specialists. We have mentioned the concept of musical sound, *nada*, and its extra-musical implications. When one moves from one such sound to the next, an interval is formed. In India, the smallest interval perceptible to the ear is called a *sruti*. Modern Karnatic musicians sometimes use this term to mean pitch in the same way that Western musicians may use, for example, the word "third" to mean both the third tone of a scale and an interval of three notes. The term *sruti*, when used to mean an interval, does not refer to a constant distance. In practice, there seem to be three kinds of *sruti*, which vary greatly in size. A theoretical average for the three sizes would be approximately 22 cents, 66 cents, and 90 cents, however, various schools of Indian music will handle them in their own way. The important point to remember is that when Indian theory speaks of 22 (or more) *sruti* to the octave, these are not equidistant intervals, as are found in the theoretical 12 tempered half steps of the Western chromatic scale.

In Indian music one cannot move from one *sruti* to an adjacent one (compare with the similar idea in Persian theory on page 49). Rather, two to four *sruti* are combined into a musical interval, a *svara*. *Svara*, like *sruti*, has the implication of both a tone and an interval, since it takes seven *svara* to arrive at a *saptaka*, a completed octave. In musical practice a given *svara* may include not only the actual note but also certain ornamentations that are part of the note in a given musical context. There are special names for the seven *svara*, but only the first syllable of each name is generally used in writing about these notes. Thus, the sounds *sa, ri, ga, ma, pa, dha*, and *ni*—like the Western *do, re, mi*—have become basic terms for discussing or singing Indian music.

When seven *svara* are played in order, a scale, *grama*, is produced. In ancient theory there were three basic *grama*, the *sa-grama*, *ma-grama*, and *ga-grama*. The *ga-grama* does not appear until the *Samgita Ratnakara* and has no practical application in India today. Exactly what the *Natya Sastra* says about the other two scales is rather controversial. It mentions the number of *sruti* in the *sa-grama* in the following order: 4 3 2 4 4 3 2. The *ma-grama* is given as: 4 3 4 2 4 3 2. The trouble is that some theorists say that these numbers are read from the top note down like the ancient Greek scales, while others say they are read from the bottom up like Western scales. Among the "bottom up" school, some begin the first interval on the note *ni* and some on *sa*. Part of the problem may be that the ancient theory was based on a cyclic system although later practice used a divisive technique. The solution of this enigma is actually philological as well as musicological, and in any case does not seriously affect an understanding of modern Indian practice. However, the concept of the two fundamental *grama* in ancient times stimulated a host of further refinements that made Indian classical theory one of the great musical syntheses of the world. Example 4-3 provides a simplified diagram of some of the major divisions of this system as it is used today. It begins by showing progressive levels of complexity and continues in a somewhat chronological fashion.

The next step in Indian theory, as illustrated, was the formation of 14 modes, *mucchanas*, created by using each of the 7 notes of the two basic scales as a starting note for a mode. Later, 7 of the resulting 14 were chosen as the most useful and were called *jatis*. By constructing modes of less than 7 notes it was possible eventually to create 11 additional *jatis*. Today the term *jatis* often refers to the classification of modes by the number of notes they contain. However, the older *jatis* as basic modes were more than just a series of notes. They began to take on special melodic characteristics as well as extramusical connotations. They were, in fact, the prototypes of the *raga*.

The term *raga* is defined as a scalar-melody form; that is, it is both the basic scale and the basic melodic structure. However, the term *raga* actually embraces most of the concepts that the Indians have thought were essential to the sound of music over many centuries. While Alain Danielou[2]

---

[2] *Northern Indian Music* (London: C. Johnson, 1949-54) 2 vols. Two extramusical aspects of the *raga* are its connections with poetry and painting. There is an important genre of Indian moghul art growing directly out of these connections.

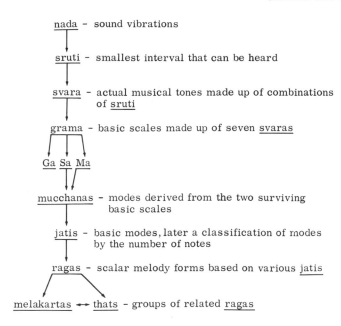

nada - sound vibrations

sruti - smallest interval that can be heard

svara - actual musical tones made up of combinations
        of sruti

grama - basic scales made up of seven svaras

Ga Sa Ma

mucchanas - modes derived from the two surviving
            basic scales

jatis - basic modes, later a classification of modes
        by the number of notes

ragas - scalar melody forms based on various jatis

melakartas ←→ thats - groups of related ragas

EXAMPLE 4-3. The Indian theoretical system in outline.

has given 15 different items that should be taken into account in defining a given North Indian *raga*, we will discuss only a few of the most essential elements found in any *raga* from either North or South India.

The actual scale of the *raga* must be shown in both its ascending and descending form, since they often differ. In addition, the notes may not proceed in an orderly manner. Many *ragas* change direction to repeat previous notes or add new tones in a quasi-melodic fashion. Also, specific notes within the *raga* will have special ornamentations (*murchanas* in the North, *gamakas* in the South). The tonic and its fifth, however, are not ornamented. In the North there are two important notes that dominate each raga: one is the *vadi*, which may or may not be the starting note (*sa*) of the scale; the other is the *samvadi*, a fourth or fifth above the *vadi*. Like the reciting tones of Gregorian chant music, these notes play important roles in the actual melodies written within a given *raga* as well as in the improvisations based upon it. While similar reciting tones appear in South Indian practice, they are not given theoretical significance as in the North. Finally, *ragas* relate to specific moods or connotations. A corollary to this is the time of day for which they are best suited.

Theoretically, thousands of *ragas* may exist. In theory books there are occasional lists of up to one thousand *ragas* actually named and described. Names of specific pieces can be found in some three hundred *ragas*. However, in either Hindustani or Karnatic practice today there are probably only about fifty *ragas* that are used with any frequency. Nevertheless, with such a large number of possibilities it is only logical that Indian theorists should organize *ragas* into related groups. For example, many *ragas* have a complementary, related scale called a *ragina*. The *ragina* is said to be the female companion of the *raga*. In addition, in North India large numbers of *ragas* and *raginas* with similar structures are organized into groups called *thats*. In South India the most important *raga* grouping is a system called the seventy-two *melakartas*. This system was based on a new theoretical approach first suggested by Venkatamakhi in 1620. It allowed new *ragas* to be produced and to be grouped with some of the older ones in a logical and consistent manner.[3] Some of the new *ragas* created by this system were incorporated into the Hindustani *that* system in the 1930's by Bhatkhande.

The grand musical concepts of the *raga* tradition continue to stimulate Indian and foreign musicians, yet the problems of scale and melody are only part of the Indian music theory picture. The other great force in Indian music is rhythm.

The Indian theory of rhythm, like that of melody, has its origin in the reciting of sacred Sanscrit texts. Thus, the basic time unit (*matra* in the North, *akshara* in the South) is defined as the shortest time in which one syllable can be pronounced. If, for the sake of analogy only, we make this basic unit equivalent to a Western quarter note it will be clear what is meant in Indian theory by the statement that this unit is a foundation for larger or smaller values—just as in the West, the half note and eighth note can be formed out of the quarter note. However, the Northern *matra* and the Southern *akshara* do not seem to be the same size. For example, the time unit called a *laghu* is defined as one *matra* in the North and as four *akshara* in the South, and the *druta* is one-half *matra*, or two *akshara*.

The core of the Indian rhythm system is the term *tala*. A *tala* consists of a rhythmic cycle (*vibhaga*) of from 3 to 128 beats marked off by accents into smaller rhythmic groups (*angas*).[4] Each *tala* is named and can be classified, like a *raga*, into a *jatis*, in this case according to the number of beats in the principal rhythmic group. Thus, Example 4-4 uses *adi tala*, which has a rhythmic cycle of eight beats (shown beneath the tune for the first two measures). The cycle is divided into three rhythmic groups of four beats, two beats, and two beats. Thus, the *tala* illustrates the *additive* approach to rhythm in which units of various size are combined, rather than the *divisive* method normally found in the even subdivisions of a measure of Western music.

Students of European medieval music will recognize the *tala* as a more

---

[3] The clearest explanation of the specific methods as well as actual charts of the *melakartas* are found in Harold Powers, *The Background of the South Indian Raga-System* (Ann Arbor: University Microfilms, 1963) I, 17-23.

[4] The term *angas* is also used to indicate tetrachord units in Indian scales.

complex version of the concept of *talea*.[5] Like the isorhythms of late medieval Europe, the *tala* can be played at various speeds within a given piece, thus changing its relation to the melody. Despite the great variety of *talas*, the most common units used today are from five to eight beats long, although the internal subdivisions are many.

Indian musicians memorize *tala* by a hand system of beating, counting, and waving. When a musician is playing, his hands are busy, but if you watch his knee or foot you will see, not the steady tapping of the Western musician's feet, but the assymetrically spaced divisions of the various rhythmic groups within the *tala*. A profound knowledge of the basic structure of the *tala* is essential for the performer because, as with the *raga*, there are further refinements built on its framework. For example, characteristic rhythms are found in each *tala* that do not emerge until an instrumentalist begins to improvise on it. Like the melodic motives of a *raga*, these rhythms are guidelines for the improvisor.

In practicing rhythms, mnemonics called *bols* are used. These are onomatopoetic versions of the basic sounds produced on Indian drums. It is possible to sing the *bols* in place of the drumming itself. The mention of this technique, however, takes us beyond the topic of theory and into the realm of Indian music practice.

Indian music practice

An Indian musician must memorize some threescore or more *ragas* and as many *talas* before he can obtain any professional status. This is done first by singing each *raga* and *tala* in an extended series of pedagogical exercises similar in structure though not in purpose to the scales and technical exercises familiar to Western music students. The object of the Western exercises is primarily instrumental technique. In India, however, they are meant to indoctrinate the student thoroughly with the possibilities of each *raga* and *tala* in order that he can get to the heart of Indian music—improvisation.

The art of Indian music has been called guided improvisation, by which is meant that at all times the musician must be guided simultaneously by the *raga* and the *tala*. In truth, all improvisation that is not merely personal musical rumination must be guided by some rules. Great freedom of improvisation is possible only when there are many rules for guidance. Jazz, for example, with its comparatively simple rules of order, is quite restricted in its improvisational scope. Progressive jazz musicians have, in fact, been seeking new rules, including some Indian concepts, in order to expand their improvisational range. The Indian musician, by contrast,

[5] See Albert Seay's *Music in the Medieval World* (Englewood Cliffs, N.J.: Prentice-Hall, Inc., 1965), pp. 133-35.

has before him such a dazzling array of rhythmic and melodic possibilities that he need never repeat himself in a lifetime of musical activity.

The Indian performer is also a creator. Like his Western counterpart, he must practice diligently the pedagogical materials of music. Such practice makes it possible for the western musician to play a given piece time after time without the slightest variation. For the Indian, however, such practice allows him to play the same *raga* in a new way every time without losing the musical characteristics that are his guides.

This important distinction in purpose results in a different kind of artist-audience relation. The knowledgeable Western audience listens for a faithful reproduction of the composer's intention and reacts to a combination of the performer's artistry and the meaningfulness of the composition. The Indian audience reacts not to the challenge of reproduction but to the performer's ability to create his own music within given bounds. In both cases, the listener must have some foreknowledge in order to appreciate the art of the performance. In the West, this consists of knowledge of the piece, the idiom, or the form. The same kinds of knowledge are useful to the Indian but, in the case of form, the intent is different. Western classical forms of the eighteenth and nineteenth centuries were constructed to introduce the listener to the basic tonalities and themes so that their development and return could be followed. Indian classical forms are designed to acquaint the listener with the *raga* and, sometimes, a basic theme while still leaving room for the performer to reveal the beauty of the theme in terms of his own imagination. Since form follows function, one can expect Indian forms to differ from those of the West.

Most Indian forms begin with a rhapsodic, free-rhythmed introduction called an *alap*. Its function is to reveal gradually the notes of the *raga* plus its special melodic characteristics. Even before these notes appear, however, one hears a drone on the pitch center of the *raga* plus its fifth. This drone is an essential element in most Indian music, for it serves as a constant reminder of the starting point of the music throughout the performer's peregrinations in the introductions and in all the sections that follow. There are usually four additional sections in a typical Indian concert piece. In South India they are called the *pallavi, anupallavi, caranam,* and *pallavi*. In North India they are the *asthai, antara, sanchari,* and *abhoga* or *asthai*. The *pallavi* presents more specific melodic themes than the *alap* and is set in the steady rhythm of a *tala*. It concentrates on exploiting the lower and middle area of the three-octave range used in Indian music. The reciting tone (*vadi*) is emphasized. In the *anupallavi* the music rises to the middle and upper octave and the *samvadi* note is prominent. The thematic material may be different. Once the upper octave is reached in the *sanchari* section, the improvisation becomes the most daring. The *abhoga* is rather like a *coda* and ends with a return to the original material or a final fanciful variation on it. Southern Indian pieces may or may not follow the same general pattern.

One must remember that during the formal progress of a piece the performer is not only playing upon the notes, ornaments, and melodic characteristics of the *raga* but may also be using a well-known melody composed by someone else. Some idea of the complexity of such pieces can be seen in Example 4-4, which shows the preliminary Karnatic flute variations (after an *alap* not shown) on the opening phrase of the composition "Sandehamunu," by the composer Tyagaraja (1767-1847). The *raga* and *tala* are shown, along with the original first phrase upon which these variations were made. The opening beats of the drum have been included to show how that instrument enters. To show the artistic manner in which the tune is varied, the subsequent phrases have been arranged in a *comparative score* in which related lines are shown immediately below the original line. This method is used in many transcriptions that involve highly varied pieces in either folk or art musics.

When more than one player is involved in Indian art music, the performance becomes something of a contest. If a drummer is used, he may try to trip up the other musicians with complicated permutations of the *tala* rhythm. The other players, of course, can play with the *tala* as well. Notice in Example 4-4 how even the composer has set the basic accents of the melody in a very subtle relation to the *tala*. A common technique of the virtuoso performer is to begin a melodic pattern on the upbeat of an unaccented beat and repeat it in such a way that its rhythm conflicts with the *tala* for three complete cycles only to land miraculously on the first beat of the fourth cycle. On such occasions one can hear a sigh of satisfaction rise from the audience. They have experienced in an art the kind of thrill we get from watching a tightrope walker execute a difficult balancing act and end with a graceful leap upright on the wire. For the traditional Indian, however, the experience has been more than a ravishing of the senses. The ethical aspects of music, mentioned earlier, are still strong. Devotional songs such as the *dhrupad* in the North and the *kirtana* in the South are the source of many performances. Some of the most famous composers, such as Tyagaraja (Example 4-4), are considered to be saints. This attitude is reflected as well in the concept of the teacher as *guru*. A traditional *guru* receives no pay for his lessons outside devotion and service. Ideally, his intent is to guide the disciple spiritually through music. As a result, professional musicians continue to burn incense before the picture of their *guru* in remembrance of their perpetual debt.

Though all Indian classical music may have a spiritual implication, it is not all necessarily religious. For example, the *javali* secular pieces are noted for their lightness. The theme and variation form known as a *gat* may be considered to be either secular or sacred, depending on the origin of the tune on which the variations are based. There are, in addition, many dance pieces, although much of Indian dance also has a religious base. The same can be said for a majority of Indian theatricals. The essence of Indian art

EXAMPLE 4-4. Karnatic flute variations transcribed from the record, *Anthologie de la musique classique de l'Inde* (Paris: Ducretet-Thomson Album 320 C 096-8), side 6, band 4. The performer is the famous Madras musician Tanjore Viswanathan. Used by permission of Pathé Marconi.

music, however, lies in the drone-based, *raga-tala*-oriented improvisations found in vocal and instrumental concert music. We need now to discuss the means to these artistic ends, the basic instruments of India.

Basic Indian instruments

From all that has been said about Indian theory and practice, one can expect three basic requirements in the construction of instruments suitable for such music. First, there must be a flexibility in pitch production and tuning in order to accommodate the many *ragas*. This is reflected in the lack of fixed-pitched metallophones and xylophones of the sort found throughout Southeast Asia and Indonesia. A second consideration is the necessity of a constant drone. This need results in a complete lack of melodic capabilities in some instruments, their sole *raison d'être* being to provide the all-important pitch orientation. Finally, the importance of rhythm in Indian music has necessitated drums as well as rhythmic devices attached to basically melodic instruments. With these three principles in mind we shall now discuss briefly the major components of India's instrumental arsenal.

There are three basic drums in Indian art music, the *mridanga* of the South and the *tabla* and *baya* of the North. The *mridanga* (Plate VII, figure 20) is a two-headed barrel drum related to the *dhol*, mentioned in our Central Asian discussion. It is laid across the lap so that both drum heads may be subjected to the subtle flights of the performer's fingers and palms. Both heads have a black paste tuning patch made of boiled rice and various powders. The patch on the left head is removed and replaced at each performance so that the tone and the actual pitch of the drum will be correct for the given situation. Similar patches are found on the single heads of the kettle-shaped *baya* (figure 21) and the *tabla* (figure 22). The traditional account of their origins says that they were created by cutting a *mridanga* in half. While their present shapes and materials would contradict this, it is true that the tuning patch on the *tabla* (played with the right hand) is permanent, while the left handed *baya* patch is removable. These two drums are always played together.

An unadorned, side-blown cane flute like the one that performed Example 4-4 is, perhaps, the most totally melodic instrument of India. The *nagasuram* (*nagasvaram*) oboe is another important Indian aerophone. It may have more than seven finger holes, the extra holes being plugged with wax to regulate the basic pitch of the instrument. It is often accompanied by the *s'ruti*, another conical double-reed that plays only the drone.

The most famous instrumental creations of India are found in the chordophones. Since instrument-making in India is still basically a hand craft, there are many local variations on any given instrument, but the instruments found in Plates VIII and IX show the basic types. On Indian chordophones, three kinds of strings may be found: melodic strings, drone strings, and sympathetic vibrators. This can be seen clearly in the evolution of the *vina*.

PLATE VII. *Indian Drums*

Fig. 20. Mridanga.

Fig. 21. Baya.

Fig. 22. Tabla.

In ancient times the term *vina* referred to a type of arched harp much like those of the ancient Near East. However, as can be seen in Plate VIII, the surviving variants of the *vina* are either zithers or lutes. Figure 23 shows the North Indian *bin*, a tube zither with two large calabash resonators; high frets; four melody strings; and three drone strings, two on one side and one on the other. The high frets make it possible to play the important ornamentations of individual notes by pressing down or pulling the strings to the side. Figure 24 shows the North Indian *bin sitar*, a trough zither. The two gourd resonators are still present, and there are varying numbers of melody and drone strings. The frets, however, are quite different, being metal rods held to the sides of the trough by gut. This arrangement makes it easier to adjust the pitches to those of a specific *raga*. This method is probably an adaptation of the movable fret systems noted earlier on many of the plucked lutes of the Near East.

The South Indian *vina* in figure 25 maintains the tradition of melody strings (four) and drone strings (three). It should be noted that the drone strings can also be used to keep track of the *tala* by stroking them in a proper rhythmic pattern. The frets are metal rods, although they are set in walls of blackened wax rather than tied with gut as in the *bin sitar*. The important difference in the Karnatic *vina* is that one of the calabash resonators has coalesced with the finger board to turn the instrument into a lute. In this case the upper gourd is basically decorative rather than functional. The carved head at the top of the instrument is somewhat functional, as it has a storage compartment within it in which a can of coconut butter is kept; this is used to lubricate the performer's fingertips as they glide over the frets. On this instrument the ornamentations are most often made by pulling the string to one side.

The North Indian *sitar* shown in figure 26 is the latest development in the *vina* family. Like the Karnatic *vina*, the *sitar* is a lute. The upper gourd is again acoustically nonfunctional, though it does help hold the neck of the instrument off the floor when it is set down. In addition to the five melodic strings and two drones, the *sitar* has a set of thirteen sympathetic vibrators. Each is tuned to a different pitch so that some will vibrate sympathetically whenever a note is played on the melody strings. These vibrators give the Hindustani *sitar* that special hollow sound familiar to devotees of Indian music. Room is made for all these strings beneath the frets by having a concave trough along the finger board and convex frets tied with gut onto the walls of the trough. These convex frets also make it easier to pull the strings when playing ornaments.

Ornaments are less easily heard on a rather rare Indian box zither, called the *svaramandala*, because of the lack of any dampening device that might help one distinguish individual tones. It is historically related and physically similar to the *kanun* (figure 19), which has the same dampening problem. (This is mentioned to illustrate the fact that not all

PLATE VIII. *Indian Plucked Chordophones*

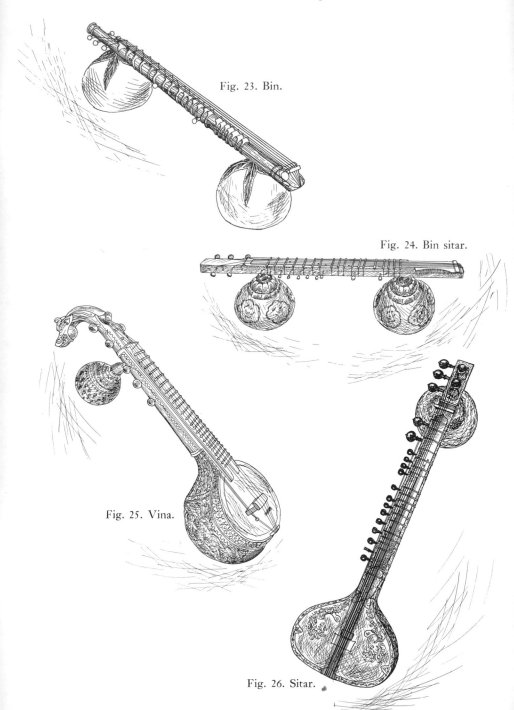

Fig. 23. Bin.

Fig. 24. Bin sitar.

Fig. 25. Vina.

Fig. 26. Sitar.

instruments in a society are chosen for their complete suitability to the idiom in which they are to perform.)

A more suitable Indian chordophone is the *sarod*, a short Hindustani lute that is either plucked or bowed. It has sympathetic vibrators and four melody strings that pass over a metal finger board. Its Islamic relations can be seen in its former name, the *rabob*. Many purely Near Eastern instruments such as the *kamanja* and *setar* are used in North India. There is one long-necked lute called the *tambura*, however, that is related to the Near East in name rather than use. Its four metal strings pass along a long neck that is round and unfretted, for the strings are only played open. The *tambura* of India is used only for drone accompaniments.

The main bowed lutes of India are the *sarangi* (figure 27), which combines melodic strings and sympathetic strings, and the *sarinda* (figure 28), which has only three melodic strings. The large indentations on the sides of both of these instruments are to accommodate the movements of the bow as it changes from string to string. Note the curious manner in which the face of the *sarinda* body is covered with membrane only on the lower half. Perhaps this construction relates to its use, for, while the *sarangi* is primarily a dance-music instrument, the *sarinda* is most often found in the hands of street musicians. As such, it is more of a folk instrument and leads us to our next topic of discussion.

Some Indian folk, popular, and theatrical music traditions

Perhaps the best-known Indian folk instrument in the West is the *pungi*, a double clarinet with the free reeds encased in a gourd. It is the actual snake charmer's instrument despite all the Western cartoon pictures of oboe-playing fakirs. However, the true world of Indian folk music, and much of its art music as well, is found in singing. The fascination of Indian art music has overshadowed folk music as an area of serious study. However, even a superficial look at Indian folk music reveals a richness worthy of the lifetime of any field collector. In the central part of India (Nagpur), in the northeastern Naga hills, and on many offshore islands there are collections of tribal peoples whose musics are more reminiscent of Arnhem Land, Borneo, and the jungles of Southeast Asia than they are of Hindu and Moslem India. Antiphonal and responsorial songs, harmonies in fourths and fifths, and even occasional singing in seconds can be found in such regions. At the same time the lovely boatmens' songs of East Pakistan and the melodies of Kashmir display casually ornamented lines based on *raga* prototypes and sung with soft-toned vocal qualities like those of Indian art music. Many Indian folk songs are sung in a rather low-ranged, intimate voice similar to that of the art music. A treasure of folk songs

PLATE IX. *Indian Bowed Lutes*

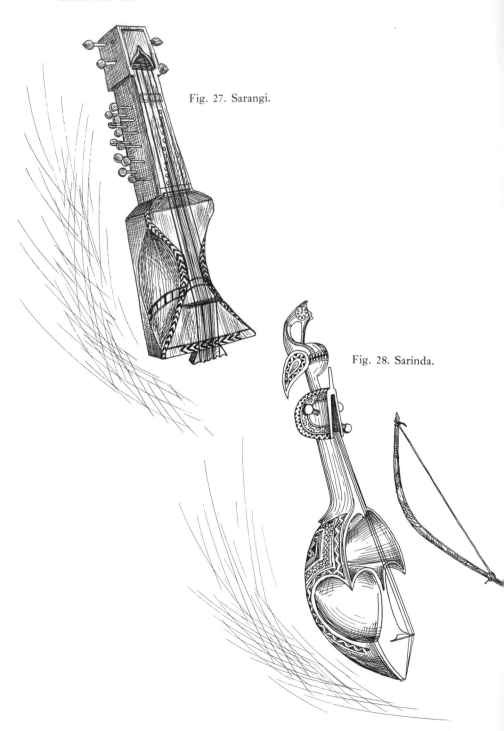

Fig. 27. Sarangi.

Fig. 28. Sarinda.

can be found in each of the hundreds of languages spoken throughout India. However, the systematic collection of this music has only recently begun, and it is hoped that more will become available in the West. At present, a search for examples of Indian songs most frequently ends up with a collection of popular tunes derived from the enormous number of Indian films produced by that huge native industry.

The relationships of Indian popular music to native and Western traditions are basically the same as those discussed earlier in connection with Near Eastern popular music (see page 57). In India, the voice tends to remain soft and low. Ornamentation is predictably reduced, though singers retain the delicate, sensual portamento sliding that is so typical of Indian singing in general. The popular orchestras lean heavily on a violin section, with native drums playing the simplest *talas* reconstituted into rumbas and beguine rhythms. In addition to many indigenous instruments and such Western substitutions as the guitar, oboe, clarinet, or muted trumpet, one often hears an Indian adaptation of the missionary harmonium, or reed organ. This instrument also is used in classical and theatrical orchestras, often with its reeds retuned to fit into the *raga* system. In popular music the harmonium, along with the various traditional instruments, is tuned in the Western tempered system. A one-note harmonium box has also been developed for use as a drone instrument.

Theatrical music of many kinds exists in India: accompaniments, on drums and cymbals, for the religious exercises at the many kinds of temples and shrines; the music of a classical dance or dance-drama form; the sounds of curved trumpets and massed drum ensembles accompanying a parade of elephants; or accompaniment for a night club routine in Bombay. We shall discuss only the first two types.

Indian theatre and dance traditionally have been connected with religious activities. This is easily seen in the Katakali dance-drama of Malabar, which originally presented its tales from the *Ramayana* and *Mahabharata* in the open-air courts of temples. The accompaniment of these pantomimes and dances consists of drums, cymbals, and narrating singers. Drums form the major part of the accompaniment for the Kandyan dances of Ceylon, which relate to the special Buddhist festivities of that island.

The orchestras are more elaborate for the accompaniment of the better-known classical dances of South India. These dances, based on the precepts of the *Bharata Natya Sastra* mentioned earlier, also have their religious undertones, for they were originally performed by temple *devadasi* girls. Today many professional concert performers still begin their careers as temple girls. A standard accompaniment for such dancing is a singer, a *mridanga* drum, and a *vina*, plus a drone instrument and perhaps a flute. Western clarinets and violins are also common. The lead singer may play the *talam*, a pair of small hand cymbals that are essential in guiding the rhythmic movements of the dancer. Rhythmic mnemonics called *sollukkatu* and Indian solmizations, in addition to poetic texts, are used by the singers.

The major form of North Indian classical dancing, Kathak, began with a more secular inspiration, the court dances of Persia as introduced by the Moghul rulers from the fourteenth century on. This tradition soon mixed with the indigenous terpsichorean art based on the *sastras*, so that today many of the important hand gestures (*mudras*) and subjects of Kathak are directly related to Indian ideals. The accompanying orchestras also show a mixture, with instruments such as the *sarangi* bowed lute and the plucked *sarod, sitar,* and *tambura* being combined with the *tabla* and *baya* drums. A singer is always present. Occasionally one can hear a set of bowls called *jalatarang*, which are tuned by filling them with different amounts of water so that complete melodies can be played by striking their edges with two thin wooden sticks. Their circular arrangement in front of the player reminds one of the drum and gong circles of Southeast Asia (see Plate X, figure 30).

Though the Kathak and Bharata Natya dancing are the heart of the Indian classical dance tradition, there are many regional and folkloric traditions that maintain independent styles. Their accompaniments can vary from bagpipes in Northern Pakistan to small bowed lutes with coconut shell bodies in Manipur. The most common instrument for such dances is the double-headed drum of the *dhol* or *dholaka* type, though many other styles can be found. One particularly interesting form is a small hourglass-shaped drum called the *damaru*, which is played by twisting it so that the knotted ends of a cord tied around its waist will strike the skins alternately. This drum is closely connected with the cult of Siva in India; variants of it are found throughout Tibet and East Asia in connection with Buddhist activities (cf. page 103).

Nationalist sentiment in South Asia has created state subsidies for many of the forms mentioned above. However, their real strength lies in the fact that, despite great efforts at modernization and Westernization, there is still a large audience in the Asian subcontinent that follows the traditional arts with interest and pride.

A theoretical postscript

As we study the various musics of the world we normally find the traditional idioms on the defensive against Western intrusions. India seems to be an exception. Western art music is hardly taught and the music of the schools is still more heavily Indian than Western. Why? A possible answer may be in the early existence of a thoroughgoing theoretical system with which the native musician could explain himself when confronted by the analytical Western mind. For most non-Western musicians, the only answer to the question "Why do you play your music in this manner?" is a shrug and a statement, "I play it thus because that's the way it's supposed to go." The professional Indian musician, like his Western counterpart, can analyze his music if necessary and show, note by note, where it comes from and "why." Perhaps what are needed in other art traditions are depth studies that will make equally explicit the rules of order underlying each system and which the traditional performers may know only subliminally. Such constructions could be dangerous misinterpretations of the traditional world; however, if correct, they could give the traditional artist a vocabulary with which to explain his music to the outside world. In India, at least, there seems to be evidence that a well-organized music theory and a flourishing performance tradition can absorb the shock of foreign confrontations without destroying themselves in the reaction.

Bibliography and discography

The basic studies of Central Asian music are in Russian. Victor Belaiev, who has published several articles (in English) in *The Musical Quarterly* (Vols. XIX, 1933, and XXI, 1953), has written the only complete summary of the area, *Ocherki Poistorii Muzyki Narodov SSSR* (Moscow; 1962, 2 vols.). Examples of the music are found in the Folkways records *Music of the Russian Middle East* (6916) and *Folk Music of the U.S.S.R.* (FE 4535). Bruno records concentrate on reconstructed folk music. The record *Afghanistan* (Musicaphon BM 30 L 2003) contains excellent recordings and photos, but suspect notes and transcriptions.

A. H. Fox Strangways' *The Music of Hindustan* (London: Oxford Press, 1914) is still the best introduction to Indian music. Arnold Bake's article and bibliography in *Ancient and Oriental Music*, Vol. I of *The New Oxford History of Music* (London: Oxford Press, 1957) is also a good starting place. An explanation of Hindustani music by a true believer is Alain Danielou's *Northern Indian Music* (London: Johnson, 1949) with one volume of theory and a second volume of music. Harold Powers' Princeton dissertation, *The Background of the South Indian Raga-system* (Ann Arbor, University Microfilms, 1963), is a brilliant explanation of the Karnatic system of vocal music along with an entire volume of transcriptions. His article, "Indian Music and the English Language," *Ethnomusicology*, Vol. IX, No. 1 (Jan., 1965), effectively reviews all the basic English writings on Indian music.

There is a large selection of Indian records available in the West. The best general collection is the Ducretet-Thomson *Anthologie de la Musique Classique de l'Inde* (320 C 096-8). The Columbia album *India* (KL 215) also contains a wide selection. Ravi Shankar has several records of *sitar* pieces on the World Pacific label, while Karnatic *vina* playing is heard on the London record *Classical Indian Music* (CM 9282); the latter includes short explanations by Yehudi Menuhin. Folkways has several offerings, of which *Music from South India Kerala* (FE 4365) is of special interest because of its harmonic examples and excerpts from Kathakali plays. *Ritual Music of Manipur* (FE 4479) contains theater music from that region. *Religious Music* (FE 4431) and *Ragas* (FE 3530) contain some transcriptions as well as good performances. Capitol records can always be relied upon for commercial music from exotic parts of the world, in this case the record *Modern Motion Picture Music of India* (T 10090).

5
Southeast Asia

Introduction

The area known as Southeast Asia encompasses the twentieth-century countries of Burma, mainland Malaysia, Singapore, Thailand, Cambodia, Laos, and Vietnam. Over the centuries the names and cultural conditions of these various areas have changed often. The magnificent ruins of Angkor Wat, for example, are a monument to only one of several brilliant kingdoms that flourished in Southeast Asia between approximately the seventh and fifteenth centuries. The jungles and mountains that surrounded these high civilizations ensured separate tribal ways, many of which have survived to the present day. The growth of colonialism and nationalism, particularly in the nineteenth and twentieth centuries, has made inroads into both indigenous worlds, but there is still much in Southeast Asia that speaks of its ancient and its tribal traditions.

The music of Southeast Asia today reflects a mixture of indigenous genius with various combinations of influence from four main external traditions: Indonesia, China, India, and, in more recent times, the West. Hybrid musics have bred further hybrids, so that today it is very difficult to separate the many interminglings and cross-influences. Southeast Asian music shows variation not only between each nation but also between geographical regions within each country. Rather than attempting to discuss subtle cross-currents like Sino-Thai and Malayo-Indonesian influences, or minor regional differences like the Khmer and Champa styles, I shall begin by discussing Southeast Asian tonal systems in general, then go on to consider the various media and kinds of music based on those systems, in the following order: 1) percussion-dominated ensembles; 2) string-dominated ensembles; 3) wind music; 4) instrumental solo and chamber music, particularly strings; 5) sacred and secular vocal music; 6) folk and tribal music; and 7) theatrical, popular, and foreign music. While these categories are not mutually exclusive, they will serve to illustrate certain cultural continuities as well as some of the variety in Southeast Asian music. For example, all the major genres rely on oral learning rather than notation, and most musics are related to or inspired by some form of theatre. However, each country has different forms of theatricals and uses different terms for the styles of music and the instruments that relate to the general Southeast Asian tradition. I have tried to pick typical examples in each of the categories given above and to mention some regional variations without pretending to include every nation's terminology or variation.

Southeast Asian tonal systems

The most famous tone system of Southeast Asia is the so-called equidistant seven-toned (heptatonic) scale. In theory these seven tones are 171.4 cents apart, but the manner in which instruments are tuned often alters the actual distance. Example 5-1 shows this equidistant tendency, which in five-line notation is indicated by a higher-than-Western fourth (in theory, 513 cents) and a lower-than-Western seventh (1026 cents, theoretically). In performance these notes give a neutral effect. Some groups that have had contact with the West tend to adjust these tones to tempered pitches. The origin of the equidistant scale is open to considerable conjecture, and at least one theorist has proposed that it is the lost *ma-grama* of ancient India.[1] Perhaps rural ensembles may provide information on the more ancient tonal systems since, like the Indonesian *gamelan*,

[1] See Alain Danielou, *La Musique du Cambodge et du Laos* (Pondichéry: Institut Français d'Indologie, 1957), pp. 2-3.

EXAMPLE 5-1. A Burmese orchestral melody transcribed from the recording, *Burmese Folk and Traditional Music* (New York: Folkways Record P 436), side 1, band 5. By permission of Folkways Records and Service Corporation.

they contain keyed instruments and gongs of rather fixed pitches. One of the most intriguing tone-system arguments of the twentieth century revolves around the tuning of a set of supposedly ancient stone keys found in Vietnam in 1949. Many things can be "proven" according to one's interpretation of the age, tuning, and function of these stones.[2]

Example 5-2 presents yet another one of the many scales found in Southeast Asia. This example has an equidistant tendency in the upper three notes but the resolutions of the neutral D-flat to C and the "gap" between B-flat and G create a totally different effect than that found in Example 5-1. This is particularly evident if one listens to the recording. To the American ear, Example 5-2 sounds surprisingly like the blues. The similarity is due to the fact that the American Negro also exploited neutral tones in his traditional music. Example 5-2, however, is a thoroughly indigenous piece.

There are seven-tone scales in Southeast Asia that concentrate on a pentatonic "core." The two notes most often de-emphasized in such scales are the fourth and the seventh. There are, of course, purely pentatonic pieces (see Example 5-3). A majority of these are of the well-known, no-half-step (anhemitonic) variety. However, even this seemingly simple scale is subject to tonal refinement. In Southeast Asia it has modal forms, under which system certain melodies that seem to use a six- or seven-note scale may actually be shifting between one five-note system and another.[3]

---

[2] A convenient summary of research on these stones is found in Curt Sachs, *The Wellsprings of Music* (The Hague: Nijhoff, 1962), pp. 106-8.

[3] Such a technique has been labeled *métabole* by Tran Van Khe in his *La Musique vietnamienne traditionnelle* (Paris: Presses Universitaires de France, 1962), p. 225.

EXAMPLE 5-2. A Cambodian wind ensemble piece transcribed from the record-ing, *Cambodia* (Kassel: Musicaphon Record BM 30 L 2002), side 1, band 7. Used by permission.

These melodic "modulations" are extremely important to the flow of music in such basically nonharmonic traditions as those of Southeast Asia. Here the forward-moving dynamism of the music is solely dependent on melodic and rhythmic tensions. This flow is further aided in Southeast Asia by the emphasis in each scale on certain "pillar tones"[4] that are

---

[4] The term was first applied to Southeast Asian music by Jaap Kunst in *Music in Java* (The Hague: Nijhoff, 1949) I, 92, 94. It is derived from the *Gerüsttöne* con-cept of early German theorists.

melodically consonant; that is, they seem to be at rest and require no further melodic resolution. Other notes in the scale are melodically dissonant or tense and seek resolution into one of the pillar tones. The notes F and C and A might be considered pillar tones in Example 5-1, while B-flat and F form the pillars for Example 5-2, the remaining tones being melodically tense and in need of further resolution.

Attempts have been made to link Southeast Asian tonal systems with those of India by comparing contemporary Indian *ragas* with specific Southeast Asian scales, particularly those used in Hindu-oriented theatrical or religious pieces. The existence of certain beliefs concerning the mood of each scale also implies such a relation. In addition, some Southeast Asian musics use special ornaments on specific notes in each scale, much like India. The Southeast Asian ornaments sometimes involve notes outside the given theoretical scale.

Similar melodic principles can be found in Western music as well as in Indian, although our theory books do not always mention them. In Southeast Asia, written theory books are rare; when existent, they tend to be reflections of Chinese or Indian theory interpreted in terms of local practice. Nevertheless, the culturally conditioned listener of the East or West uses an aggregate of tonal and aesthetic principles, like those mentioned above, as clues that help him respond to the artistry of the music. The average native listener is, of course, only subliminally aware of such principles. For the foreign listener, a conscious awareness of their existence is a great help in learning what to listen for in the music. One of the brightest sounds with which to start such listening is found in the percussion ensembles of Southeast Asia.

Percussion-dominated ensembles

The best-known percussive ensemble in Southeast Asia is the Thai *pi phat* band. *Pi phat* ensembles vary from 6 to 14 players. A standard instrumentation includes paired idiophones which, like the sets of 3 *saron* and *gender* in the Javanese *gamelan*, have different ranges. The 21 wooden keys of the *ranat ek* xylophone (Plate X, figure 29) carry the main melodic load, assisted in a lower register by its 17-keyed companion, the *ranat thum*. Their metal-keyed counterparts are the 21-keyed *ranat ek lek* (or sometimes *ranat thong*) and the 17-keyed *ranat thum lek* xylophones.

Circles of knobbed gongs (Plate X, figure 30) are essential to most of the percussion ensembles of Southeast Asia. In Thailand there are two forms, the lower-pitched, 16-gong *khong wong yai* and the higher 17- or 18-gong *khong wong lek*, of which the two lowest-pitched gongs are nonfunctional. Two kinds of cymbals are also found in a *pi phat*. The smaller ones (*ching*) resemble the small dance-orchestra cymbals of India,

PLATE X. *Southeast Asia* (*Thailand*)

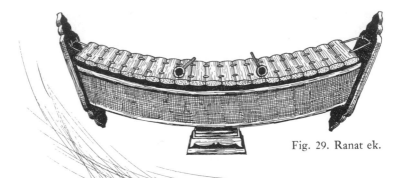

Fig. 29. Ranat ek.

Fig. 30. Khong wong yai.

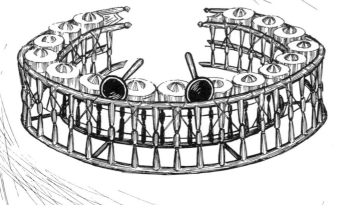

Fig. 31. Pi nai.

while the larger (*chap*) are like the knobbed cymbals found in the Buddhist rituals of Tibet and China. Along with a hanging knobbed gong (*khong mong*) they provide a colotomic structure. Two kinds of drums also assist in this function. One is a large, laced-head barrel drum called the *tapone*, both heads of which are played with the hands. The other is a pair of tacked-headed barrel drums played with sticks, called the *glong that*. Tuning paste is applied to the heads of both types of drums.

The only instrument that keeps the *pi phat* from being completely percussive is the *pi nai* oboe (Plate X, figure 31). This instrument is novel in several ways. Its bulging shape is totally different from the standard *sornay-zurna* type found elsewhere in the world or in other ensembles of Southeast Asia (compare figure 31 with figure 18). It can be tuned by extending its thick teakwood body with a rim of wax at the lower end. The most novel feature of the *pi nai*, however, is its reed, which is not the standard double but rather quadruple. Four short rounded reeds made of dried palm leaf are bound to a metal tube inserted at the top of the instrument. These reeds are set in a vertical rather than the standard horizontal position and the set is "swallowed," that is, it is placed within the mouth cavity rather than on the lips. The reason for the novel vertical placement is that the tongue can then touch the edges of the vibrating reeds and stop some of them, thus allowing the player to produce different octaves of sound with only six finger holes.

The Cambodian and Laotian *pi phat* ensembles are similar in instrumentation to the group just described. All three groups are best heard in the royal palaces, where they accompany the official ceremonies and classical dramatic presentations. Some private academies of ensemble playing also exist, as do various rural orchestras. However, this music is derived primarily from the days of courtly power and, unlike the Indonesian *gamelan*, has little support among the populace except as it is used to accompany public theatricals.

The Burmese percussion orchestra (*saing waing ah-pwe*) has deeper roots, perhaps because it is more itinerant and travels from village to village in support of the public theatre (*pwe*). This orchestra, sometimes called merely a *saing* or *saing waing*, derived its name from its most novel instrument, a set of twenty-one tuned drums (*saing waing*). These are hung on an ornate circular screen which, while partially hiding the performer from view, adds a decorative visual pleasure to the performance. Such an interest in the visual appeal of instruments is characteristic of most Southeast Asian instrumental traditions, and the nonfunctional parts of many instruments are overlaid with traceries and color.

The rest of the Burmese ensemble consists of a circle of twenty-one knobbed gongs (*kyi waing*); a large hanging barrel drum (*segi*), large and small cymbals (*ya gwin* and *si*); two long bamboo clappers (*wa let kyong*); and a double-reed aerophone (*hne*) with a conical bore and a very large, loose, metal bell. Example 5-1 is an excerpt from a *saing* ensemble. Like all the other orchestras of Southeast Asia, the various melodic instruments in this ensemble create a kind of stratified polyphony.

The description of various percussion ensembles and their functions in Southeast Asia brings to mind the Indonesian *gamelan*. The prevalence of melodic idiophones and knobbed gongs as well as the close connections of the music with dance and drama are reminiscent of the *gamelan*. However, since few of the Southern Asian melodic idiophones are capable of sustaining long tones (as can the Indonesian *saron* and *gender*), their melodic style is much more incisive. The Burmese excerpt in Example 5-1 shows a tendency for short-breathed lines with sudden changes in melodic direction. Melodies from other Southeast Asian ensembles tend to be equally fast and florid, though their phrases may be longer and more isometric than those shown in Example 5-1.

String-dominated ensembles

The *mahori* bands of Thailand and Cambodia and the *seb noi* of Laos are called string ensembles because they emphasize bowed and plucked chordophones, though many other instruments are included in them. The generic terms for these bowed instruments are *saw* in Laos and Thailand, and *tro* in Cambodia and among the Mons of Burma. There are three basic kinds of bowed chordophones in such groups; they will be described in their Thailand forms.

The first type is a three-stringed spiked fiddle called the *saw sam sai*. Both its shape and its separate bow relate it to the *rebab* (see Plate III, figure 8). The second type is the *saw duang*. Its two strings lie one above the other, vertical to the body, like those of the Chinese *hu ch'in* (Plate XIII, figure 38), rather than horizontal like the strings of a Western violin, since the bow passes between the strings rather than over them as with the *rebab* or the violin. The body of the *saw duang* is cylindrical and open, like that of the *hu ch'in* in figure 38. The third type of bowed string instrument, the *saw u*, is like the *saw duang* except that the body is usually made of half a coconut shell. Other Chinese-style bowed chordophones with four strings and coconut shell or cylindrical shaped bodies also exist in Southeast Asia.

The basic styles of bowed lutes described above are graphic illustrations of the confrontation of East and West in Southeast Asia; when the string pegs are inserted from the rear, the influence is clearly that of China, while lateral pegs mean a Moslem or Western origin. The term Western has been added because the violin, played in the vertical *rebab* position, can often be found in Southeast Asian ensembles. A good example is in the orchestra of the Mon people in Burma. Though historically the ancient Mons seem to have used only percussion instruments, their present orchestras include two three-stringed fiddles with violin bodies; the crocodile zither (figure 6); two small drums; and an end-blown flute.

Among the plucked chordophones of Southeast Asian ensembles the Thai *chakay* (Plate II, figure 7) is of particular interest since it is related to similar instruments already familiar to us from the Philippines (*kachapi*), Borneo (*kudyapi*), and Java (*kachapi*). India also figures in its history, for the manner in which the *chakay's* three gut strings pass over high frets is reminiscent of the *vina*, though the sound produced is less resonant and the *chakay* playing style less florid. A zoomorphic variant of it is the *chakey* or *mi gyaun* (Plate II, figure 6) of the Burmese Mon orchestra.

Another plucked chordophone found in *mahori* groups is the *grajappi* lute. This instrument has four strings in double courses and a long fretted neck whose thin, curved line forms a lovely visual image. The Cambodians make greater use of this instrument under the name *chapey-thom*.

To these strings are added various xylophones, circle gongs, cymbals, drums, and end-blown flutes to make up standard *mahori* orchestras. One drum of particular interest is the single-headed pot-shaped *thon* or *thap*, which resembles the Near Eastern *tombak*. The main functions of *mahori* orchestras are to accompany songs and plays. Like the *pi phat*, they find their main patronage in the capitals, although individual bowed instruments are widespread rurally.

Wind ensembles and instruments

The most famous wind ensemble of Southeast Asia consists of a group of *khaen* (*can* or *khen*). As seen in Plate XI, figure 32, the *khaen* is itself a kind of ensemble since it can play chords and melody at the same time. It consists of from 6 to 16 long bamboo pipes (40 to 80 inches) joined in the center or bottom by a single wind chamber. Each pipe contains a single free reed that sounds when a hole on the side of the pipe is closed. The harmonic, melodic, and drone aspects of *khaen* music can be seen in Example 5-3. Nasal breathing allows the performer to keep the air chamber

EXAMPLE 5-3. A Thai *khaen* piece transcribed from the recording, *Music of Thailand* (New York: Folkways Record FE 4463), side 1, band 1. By permission of Folkways Records and Service Corporation.

filled and thus maintain the sound. When *khaen* play in ensembles the separate parts are primarily for reinforcement rather than for the addition of new polyphonic lines. The *khaen* is believed to have originated in Laos but, as we saw in Borneo (page 24), is widespread throughout South Asia. In addition to being the predecessor of the Chinese *sheng* (Plate XII, figure 37), it may also be a distant precursor of the Western organ. In any event, it is one of the more complicated and widespread folk instruments of Southeast Asia. In its folk form, the pipes may stick out of one side (like the *sheng*, figure 37) rather than penetrate the gourd.

A variety of both horizontal and end-blown flutes exists in Southeast Asia. The latter include open-end and closed-end notched flutes as well as block flutes. In Thailand they all tend to fall under the term *khlui*. The Thai block flute is perhaps the best-known ensemble aerophone, since it appears frequently in *mahori* orchestras. The opening of the block is at the back of the instrument rather than at the front (as on the Western recorder). In addition to six finger holes, it has one hole that is covered with a thin membrane to create a soft buzzing sound.

Another important aerophone found in ensembles as well as in solo music is the *pi saw*, also called sometimes a *khlui*. A relative of the *khaen*, it consists of a single free reed placed near the closed end of a long bamboo pipe in which six or seven finger holes have been drilled. The reed portion of the pipe is placed inside the mouth, which acts as a wind chamber. This instrument has a soft, clarinet-like tone and produces a pleasant buzzing resonance. It is commonly used for evening serenades in the villages. It can be heard in the Laotian magician's ensemble piece shown in Example 5-2.

String instrumental solo music and chamber music

One of the most lovely instrumental solo traditions of Southeast Asia is that of the *saung kauk* harp of Burma (Plate XI, figure 33). It is used in classical music to accompany the simple *cho* songs as well as several more esoteric types such as the *yodaya*. The latter are based on a Thai style of song and use a different tuning, rhythmic mode, and melodic style from those of the *cho* songs. The tuning of the harp is changed by twisting the braids that attach its 14 (formerly 13) strings to the pole. The rhythmic changes can best be heard by following the sounds of a pair of small hand bells (*si*) and a clapper (*wa*), which keep the beat much like the *talam* cymbals of India. Melodic differences in harp music can be found by studying the various principles of modes and modulations discussed earlier in this chapter as they apply to these two Burmese traditions. The extended instrumental interludes of the Burmese harp songs reveal a great interest in melodic variation and extension.

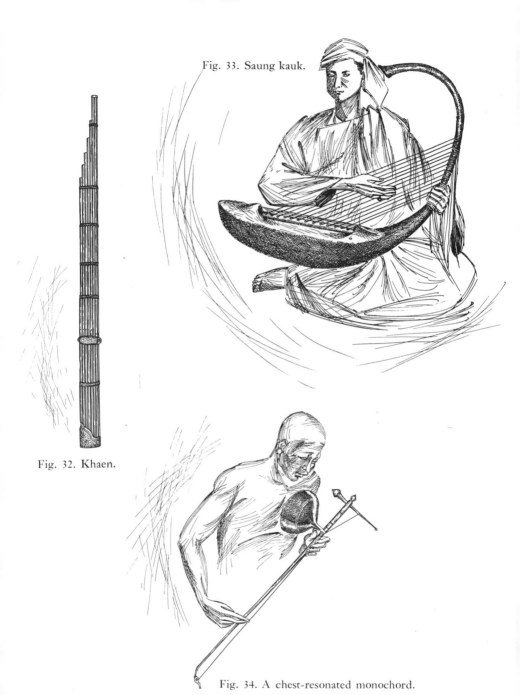

PLATE XI. *Southeast Asia*

Fig. 33. Saung kauk.

Fig. 32. Khaen.

Fig. 34. A chest-resonated monochord.

The origins of the Burmese harp have been traced to ancient India, but the living tradition of Burmese harp music is now unique in Asia. The audiences who sit all night in a Buddhist temple compound to hear it, as well as the rows of young ladies at the National Music Institute in Rangoon who diligently practice it in ensemble, are, perhaps, only faintly aware of how rare this music is. If it survives Burma's period of modernization, it will be one of the last classical harp traditions remaining from the ancient world.

Many of the instruments of the classical orchestras of Southeast Asia have a solo literature. The Mon *mi gyaun* and the Thai *chakay* and *grajappi* are good examples. However, much of the solo and chamber music of this area is really an arrangement or accompaniment of vocal music.

One of the most exotic solo strings used to accompany the voice is the monochord called in Thailand the *phin nam tao* (Plate XI, figure 34). As seen in the drawing, the resonance of the instrument is enhanced by placing the open back of its hemispherical body against the singer's chest. A similar instrument is found in Africa. In Vietnam, there is a monochord called the *dan doc huyen* or *dan bau* that uses a standard wooden body as a resonator but stretches its string between the body and a flexible vertical stick. The pitch is varied by pulling the stick sideways to increase or lessen the tension on the string, somewhat in the manner one plays tunes on a rubber band. The monochords, plus many of the other strings of Southeast Asia, have their basic repertoire in the courting music and other social music of the villages. They have been joined in recent decades by the guitar and other Western instruments.

Outside the West, the border line between orchestral and chamber music is very indistinct, for, as we have seen, many "orchestral" pieces can be played by rather small ensembles. However, one can find in Southeast Asia separate repertoires of pieces specifically created for ensembles of two or three people; this can truly be called chamber music, although the relation of parts, as with the larger groups, is basically heterophonic. One lovely example is the Vietnamese trio consisting of a two-stringed pear-shaped guitar (*ty ba*), a flute (*dich*), and a sixteen-stringed plucked zither (*tranh*). This trio, like much of Vietnam's music, reflects a strong Chinese influence.

Sacred and secular vocal music

We have already noted that much Southeast Asian instrumental music is used for vocal accompaniment. In addition, there is a rich heritage of narrative musics not directly connected with theatricals. Some are purely vocal, such as the Thai *say pha*, in which the performer accompanies himself with only four sticks clicked together like castanets. Other narrators use stringed instruments for ostinato-like backgrounds.

As in the Near East, poetry may be recited in a musical fashion, though such performances are not classified as music in Southeast Asia. However, unaccompanied praise songs sung by female attendants of the courts are considered to be music. Unison choral singing can be heard in some *mahori* pieces. Massed singing is heard most often, however, in the religious chanting of the courts and temples as well as in the theatrical music. The majority of these chants are, like most liturgies, *centric melodies;* that is, they center around one tone while using other tones to surround it. Chinese influence is strong in most Buddhist music in Southeast Asia, while many Hindu chants in Pali reveal a base in either *ragas* or in the Vedic chant tradition. The most characteristic indigenous religious music of Southeast Asia is found in the dream songs of the village clairvoyants. Personal problems of life and love are presented to these seers, who go into a trance and then through song bring back the advice of the supernatural. When we come to such music we are touching on our next topic—folk music.

Folk and tribal music

The dream songs mentioned above are found throughout Southeast Asia in the urban, rural, and back country areas. In general, as one moves into the jungles, unaccompanied vocal music becomes more prevalent. Tribal music is no respecter of modern national boundaries, and little can be said at present about the many different styles of music that exist behind the jungle wall. This, however, reflects on our lack of knowledge rather than on any lack of variety. The very functions of some tribal music are enough to tempt one into studying this area. For example, among the Pwo Karen people of North Thailand funeral songs are important socially, since funerals offer the best opportunity for young men and women to meet and flirt.

There are throughout the jungles of Southeast Asia many forms of drums. Single-laced heads and hourglass or extended, pot-shaped bodies are most frequent. Panpipes, flutes, bamboo trumpets, and folk forms of the *khaen* mouth organ are also widespread. Chinese-inspired plucked lutes are common in the northern tribes. As in Borneo, the most prized instrument seems to be the knobbed gong. One also finds occasionally a flat-surfaced gong with wide, slightly concave sides. Though suspended and played as a gong, it is derived from an ancient Chinese bronze drum.

The lullabies, love songs, and work songs of Southeast Asia lean heavily on the whole-step pentatonic scale. The kind of voice quality with which they are sung varies from a very high-pitched nasal sound to a rather soft, low crooning. In general, the higher, more tense voice qualities reflect classical influence.

Rural instrumental music is best heard in serenades and in folk dance accompaniments. The rural dances, such as the *rongen* of Malaysia, are often in quadrille form, like those of the Philippines or rural England and America. Both these quadrilles and the various couple social dances differ from their Western counterparts in several ways. The couples seldom touch (a technique favored in Euro-American social dancing since the Rock-and-Roll movement of the 1950's). Movement is primarily in the feet and torso (rather than according to the Western preference for hips) and in delicate hand gestures derived from classical dance traditions. Finally, the musical accompaniment may be quite different, though Western instrumentation is not uncommon today. In the case of the *rongen*, the accompaniment is often a violin or *rebab* plus an Arab-style pot drum. Such mixtures of instruments are frequent in Malaysia, where all the traditions of Southeast Asia plus those of India, China, the West, and the Near East have flourished through foreign settlements as well as intermixed populations. Similar mixtures may occur in the popular and theatrical traditions of all urban areas of Southeast Asia.

Theatrical, popular, and foreign music

Theatrical music in Southeast Asia has a long tradition going back to the dance dramas depicted in ancient stone reliefs. We have already shown that the *pi phat* and *mahori* ensembles can be used to accompany the modern versions of these old classical dramas. The close relationship between most Southeast Asian ensembles and drama is nicely illustrated by the division of orchestras in Burma into the *zat pwe* for secular entertainment and the *yokthe pwe* for puppet theatre music. Indeed, in all of Southeast Asia it is difficult to speak of purely instrumental music, though the theatre music can be played in concert.

Today most of the theatrical traditions of Southeast Asia have been heavily influenced by foreign production methods and musics. This is particularly true of popular comic theatres where Western and Chinese instruments predominate. One of the few public ensembles that seem to have resisted this trend is the combination of a drummer and an oboe player, who accompany the foot- and fist-swinging boxers and cock fights.

The popular and movie music of Southeast Asia shows the kind of Western influence we have seen elsewhere. While the tunes tend to be pentatonic, the accompaniment leans heavily on saxophones, trumpets, and triadic chords. Some of the courts enhance this process by an active interest in Western jazz along with the usual support of resident military bands. In the midst of such straight adoptions, one can find occasional examples of native influence. When one hears, for example, a piano played in the manner of a native xylophone, there is hope that all the Western importations have not as yet deadened the native to the charms of his own indigenous styles.

Bibliography and discography

A thorough study of a Southeast Asian music is Tran Van Khe's *La Musique Vietnamienne Traditionelle* (Paris: Presses Universitaires de France, 1962). U Khin Zaw has outlined his tradition in "Burmese Music" in *Perspective of Burma*, an *Atlantic Monthly Supplement* (1958). Alain Danielou provides a useful survey in *La Musique du Cambodge et du Laos* (Pondichéry: Institut Français d'Indologie, 1957). A detailed study by an American scholar is David Morton's *The Traditional Instrumental Music of Thailand* (Ann Arbor: University Microfilms, 1964). Dr. Morton also translated Dhanit Yupho's *Thai Musical Instruments* (Bangkok: Dept. of Fine Arts, 1960). Judith Becker, a specialist in Burmese harp music, has written a straightforward analytical study of one tribal tradition in "Music of the Pwo Karen of Northern Thailand," *Ethnomusicology*, VIII, No. 2 (May, 1964).

Folkways Records has produced *Folk and Traditional Music of Burma* (FE 4436) and is planning another Burmese release. Other Folkways offerings are *Music from South Asia* (FE 4447), *Temiar Dream Music* (FE 4460), *Music of Vietnam* (FE 4352), and *Music of Thailand* (FE 4463). The Musicaphon records *Laos* (BM 30 L 2001) and *Cambodia* (BM 30 L 2002) are the best for classical traditions and include useful photographs.

6
East Asia

Tibet

Locked in its mountain fastness, Tibet has often seemed to Westerners to be the very symbol of an ancient, unchanging, Shangri-La world. Historically, however, the culture of Tibet has been periodically changed by influences from India, China, Mongolia, and the West. Before the entrance of Indian Buddhism in the seventh century, there seems to have been an indigenous religion called *bon* whose music influenced the newer tradition and may still survive in Tibetan shaman traditions.

Tibet's characteristic Lamaistic form of Buddhism flourished during the ninth and tenth centuries, and at least one source of that time (the *Mahavyutpatti*) mentions the musical instruments used in its rituals. There are also hints in other writings that the *tala* and *raga* concepts of India were known in Tibet. New Buddhistic influences in the sixteenth century, and heavy political involvements with China in the seventeenth, produced further information on Tibetan music in Chinese commentaries.

Later, Western visitors provided scattered comments on Tibetan music; Westerners also introduced the military band to Tibet. However, in all the writings on Tibet, native or foreign, the main topic of interest has been religious music—as well it might be in a country whose theocracy has survived into the twentieth century. Thus we first turn our attention to the religious music of Tibet.

The core of Tibetan religious music is chanting, generally done on a low pitch. In group chanting each priest seeks his own tonal level rather than attempting to sing in unison with his brethren. This does not mean that the melodies are haphazard. Many are written in a *neumatic* notation —that is, a notation that uses single signs (neumes) to stand for a group of notes.[1]

Tibetan chanting can be accompanied by a variety of instruments, the simplest being the *dril-bu* hand bell. This bell is found in all Buddhist countries, its shape remaining amazingly consistent from Ceylon and Bali to China and Japan. Another common Tibetan idiophone is a pair of cymbals either large (*sil-snyan*) or small (*rol-mo*).

Among the several membranophones of Tibetan religious music, two are characteristic. One is the *lag-na*, a large, two-headed tacked barrel drum set on the end of a pole which the player grips as he beats on one head with a curved stick. The other is the *rnga-ch'un*, an hourglass-shaped drum made of two attached hemispheres often made of human skull craniums. Two strips of cloth with knobs or knots at the end are attached to the waist of the drum so that the knobs strike alternate heads when the drum is twisted back and forth in the hand. Shamans often use this instrument.

The most spectacular Tibetan ritual instruments are long, copper *rag-dung* trumpets. These straight, conically bored natural horns vary in length from some five to twenty feet. Many are made in sections that can be telescoped for portability. Each horn has a fairly shallow cup mouthpiece and, like the Western bugle, is capable of producing different tones. The basic use of these horns, however, is not to play fanfares but rather to provide a drone for the chanting. This drone is sometimes in thirds or fifths. The smaller hand trumpets have dragon heads at the bell end; the players of these also tend to concentrate on one note, from which they slide up and down. The shamans of Tibet use short trumpets made of human leg-bones. Criminals' bones are preferred because of their closer connection with Tibet's many devils, which need to be placated. The conch-shell trumpet is also found in Tibet.

[1] The other two common forms of notation are *graphic*, which indicates the height of pitches (as in our five-line staff), and *tablature*, which indicates notes or fingering on an instrument. The latter is common in China and Japan.

The only melodic instrument in Tibetan religious orchestras is the double reed *surna*, also known as the *harib* or, in the monasteries, as the *rgya-glin*. It plays preludes and interludes to the chants rather than the chants themselves.

The best opportunity to hear Tibetan music in all its splendor is during the annual *ch-ham* festival. For three days, actors in gorgeous costumes and fearsome *papier maché* heads perform an involved religious dance-drama to the accompaniment of a variety of instrumental combinations chosen primarily from the instruments listed above.

Technically speaking, the ensembles used for such public affairs are considered to be civil orchestras, while the private Lamaistic ceremonies use religious orchestras. Though there seem to be more oboes and drums in the civil groups, the general structure of the two musics tends to be the same, with alternations of percussion-accompanied singing and instrumental interludes.

Besides the great religious dramas, there are also secular dance plays and historical plays in Tibet. Their accompaniment consists of drums and cymbals. As in other traditional theatres, female actors are not used.

So far no string instruments have been mentioned, because they are not used in Tibetan religious music. In secular music, one finds a four-stringed, bowed *gophong* modelled after the Mongolian horse-head fiddle (see p. 106). Example 6-1 contains two songs accompanied by the *dram snyan*, a plucked lute with six strings in double courses tuned in thirds. Some scholars consider this instrument a link between the Far East and the ancient Near East. As used in these Tibetan folk dance examples, the *dram snyan* creates a triadic, isometric ostinato. In Example 6-1, the singers produce a stepwise heterometric melody against this.

While most Tibetan folk songs use the whole-step pentatonic scale, the two excerpts in Example 6-1 show that other, quite different tonal systems also appear. Example *a* makes striking use of the tritone (G to D-flat) and exploits harmony in seconds at each cadence. Example *b* shows a melody built basically in a chain of thirds[2] (G to B-flat to D to F) in a manner quite different from Example *a*. In both songs the tonal vocabulary of the singers seems to be independent of that of the instrument. This curious bitonality is common in many folk dances accompanied by both voices and instruments. Since researchers have had to rely primarily on materials from border peoples, caravans, and refugees coming out of Tibet, little can be said about what might be idiomatic of Tibetan folk style. There does seem to be a frequent use of antiphonal singing in dance pieces, such as Example 6-1. As yet, the space age still knows little about the music of the land nearest the sky.

[2] For a discussion of melody building through various interval chains, see Curt Sachs, *The Wellsprings of Music* (The Hague: Nijhoff, 1962), pp. 143-67.

EXAMPLE 6-1. Two Tibetan folk dance excerpts from the recording, *Songs and Music of Tibet* (New York: Folkways Record FE 4486), side 1, bands 5 and 2 (fourth entrance). By permission of Folkways Records and Service Corporation.

Mongolia

If we move down from the mountains of Tibet and out onto the steppes and deserts along China's western border, we find the tribal remnants of the Mongol Empire. In ancient times, these hardy horsemen made their fame in the art of war rather than music; but even in war, drums and bugles were used for signalling. In the thirteenth century Marco Polo mentions a battle in which both sides sang before fighting began. The signal for the start of the battle was given on a large kettle drum with the familiar name of *nagarah* (see *naqqara*, page 45).

Although these nomadic people were strong militarily, the Mongols were always susceptible to outside cultural influences. Today their western tribes are influenced by Islamic culture, while Lamaistic Buddhism and Chinese culture dominate in the East. Their indigenous shamanistic tradition survives in a few songs found in present collections, though the shaman and his drum can best be found further north in Manchuria and Siberia, as well as across the Bering Straits in Alaska and Canada.

The musical legacy of the Mongols is found today primarily in its folk music, known generically as *duun*. This music can be divided into several types of songs according to subject matter such as: spiritual songs, songs about the heroic deeds of the days of the great Khans, contemporary political songs, and epic narratives (*uliger*). While the political songs tend to be sung in unison chorus, the most common Mongolian performance practice is to use one singer who accompanies himself on the *khil-khuur* bowed lute. This fiddle has a flat trapezoid body with sheepskin covering both the front and back. It has two strings tuned in fifths. The peg box is often topped with the carving of a horse's head in a manner similar to the *gusle* of the Yugoslavian balladiers.

There seem to be two common styles of folk singing in Mongolia. One is in an even *tempo giusto*, usually isometric; the other is in a *parlando-rubato* style. In both styles, the relation of the voice to the accompaniment tends to be heterophonic. The *parlando-rubato* pieces make extensive use of melismatic improvisations in both the vocal and instrumental parts. Thus, though the songs tend to be strophic, there is considerable variation between each strophe. In the study of such variant strophic music it is often useful to construct a comparative score;[3] in this way one can quickly see the areas of similarity and difference. No notation, however, can successfully symbolize the low yodel (ululation) that is characteristic of the Mongolian manner of singing these songs.

In Mongolian music one finds a few Central Asian plucked lutes, plus Chinese-style violins and flutes. With the increase of government controls in both Chinese and Outer Mongolia during the mid-twentieth century, there has been a tendency to form State Folk Ensembles whose music seems more reminiscent of Rimsky-Korsakov than of the great Khans. However, there are still Mongolian bards practicing their solo art. Though they may now sing about the new ponies on the collective farm, there is much of the Asian steppes tradition left in their performance style.

[3] See above, p. 75, and Example 4-4. Mongolian songs in comparative scores are found in Ernst Emshiemer, *The Music of the Mongols*, Publication 21, VIII, Part 4 of *The Sino-Swedish Expedition*, Dr. Sven Hedin, director (Stockholm: Thule, 1943), 22-35.

China

Introduction. Organized civilizations of Mongoloid peoples have occupied the Chinese mainland continuously since at least 3000 B.C. By the time of their first verified dynasty, the Shang (1766-1122 B.C.), they were already using a writing system that, unlike the ancient scripts of the Egyptians and the Sumerians, related directly to the system used by their modern descendents. Thus, one finds in China a tradition of amazing age and continuity which, with the great interest in history and respect for the written word, has left a vast legacy of information about the ways of Chinese civilization over a period of some three thousand years of actual history, plus another two or three thousand years of legend and pseudo-history. Within the thousands of volumes of ancient Chinese history, philosophy, and literature that have survived to the present day, there are many scattered references to music. A composite of these sources gives us many details concerning the history, theory, instrumentation, and uses of music throughout the ages. Unfortunately, it tells us nothing about the sound of ancient Chinese music. Thus, both Western and Oriental scholars tend to concentrate on the history of Chinese music to the neglect and often the disparagement of its living tradition. This survey, reflecting the historical orientation of available material, is organized into four general periods: the formative (the third millennium B.C. through the fourth century A.D.); the international (fifth century through the ninth); the national (the tenth through the nineteenth centuries); and the period of world music (the twentieth century). The first section deals primarily with the theoretical foundations of Chinese music; sections of the second and most of the third periods will concentrate on history; only in materials since the seventeenth century will we begin to say something about the actual music. Compared to the scope of Chinese history this last section is a tiny period, though placed against the history of Western music it would cover the time from Bach to the present. An overview of Chinese music is obviously a study for a lifetime, but perhaps some of the grandeur of its history and the richness of its surviving traditions can be discerned in the discussions that follow.

The Formative Period (third millennium B.C. to fourth century A.D.). The earliest musical artifacts in China date from around 1000 B.C.; they consist of rounded clay ocarinas and stone chimes. Instruments of less durable material no doubt existed before this time, but the oldest Chinese writings list only a few of the instruments of the early Chou period (1122-221 B.C.). These writings also mention folk festivals, for ancient China seemed always to be interested in ceremonies, particularly those dealing with divination and the honoring of ancestors. Thus it is not surprising that one of the first extensive discussions of music is found in the second century B.C. *Book of Rites.* The other famous Chinese classics of this period dealing with history and court activities also contain scattered references to music, while the poetry collection, the *Book of Odes,* has many texts that seem, originally, to have been sung. The teachings of Confucius (551-479 B.C.) likewise make frequent mention of music, primarily because, like the philosophers of other ancient civilizations, Confucius considered the performance of music to be an ethical as well as pleasurable experience. From all these sources four basic kinds of information emerge: 1) the mythological origins of music; 2) the theoretical basis of Chinese music; 3) the instruments of the court; and 4) the relation of music to court life and ritual in the Chou and later the Han (third century B.C. to 220 A.D.) dynasties. These four areas will form the basis of our discussions of the foundations of Chinese music.

The most famous legend concerning the origin of Chinese music says that around 2697 B.C. a certain Ling Lun was sent by an emperor, Huang-ti, to the western mountains to cut bamboo pipes (*lü's*) from which the fundamental pitches of music could be derived. The legend is interesting in three respects. First, it places the origins of music at the western borders, where so many other new ideas have crossed over into China. Secondly, the concern of the emperor to secure proper fundamental pitches reflects indirectly the close relationship of early Chinese music to ritual and the extra-musical, for, in China, setting a proper pitch meant literally putting music in tune with the various forces of the universe. Further proof of this relationship is seen in the fact that a new emperor traditionally ordered his musicians and astrologers to work together on re-calculating the length of the imperial pitch pipes so that his reign would harmonize with all the elements of nature and supernature. This reflection of the natural order of the universe in the arts remained fundamental to Chinese music speculations until very recent times.

The third point of interest that stems from the legend of the *lü's* is that Chou and Han dynasty writers used these pipes as the basis for an elaborate tone system that still strongly influences Chinese music. The Near Eastern and Indian tone systems studied earlier were *divisive,* that is, they were based on the divisions of a vibrating string (on the *ud* and *vina* respectively). The Chinese system, by contrast, was *cyclic.* It was created from a cycle of tones generated by blowing across the tops of a set of tubes closed at one end (like a bottle), whose lengths were arranged in a set mathematical proportion.

The pitch produced by the first tube was called the Yellow Bell (*huang chung*). This does not mean it was played on a bell; it was merely a name for that pitch—as, for example, the tone vibrating 440 times a second is called in the West "A." For the sake of comparison with other material in this book, we shall call the Yellow Bell pitch middle C, though traditionally it is placed on the F above that. Additional tones are produced by constructing tubes that are alternately ⅔ and ⅓ the length of their previous tube. The acoustical basis for this method is the principle of the *overblown fifth*—that is, by blowing hard on the first tube, a tone one fifth higher (G in our series) is produced. A tube ⅓ *shorter* than the first one will produce this G without overblowing. If this second tube is overblown, the note D appears in an upper register, as shown in Example 6-2. The note D is played more easily an octave lower on a pipe ⅓ *longer*

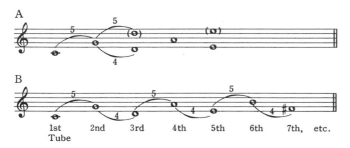

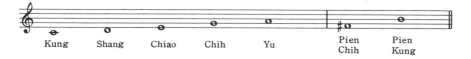

EXAMPLE 6-2. The Chinese *lü* system.

than the second pipe. A pipe ⅓ shorter than the D pipe produces an A, and a pipe ⅓ longer than the A pipe produces an E at the lower octave. When these tones are written in the manner in which they were generated, one sees that they follow a pattern going up a fifth and down a fourth, as shown in Example 6-2. Chinese theoreticians first carried this process through twelve tubes, but only the first five were needed to illustrate the fundamental five tones (*wu sheng*) of Chinese music. This pentatonic scale—which no doubt existed in China long before Chinese science found

EXAMPLE 6-3. The basic Chinese scale system and its changing tones.

a way of explaining its origin—is shown in Example 6-3, along with the Chinese names for each scale degree. These names—like the Western *do, re, mi*—indicate positions in the scale rather than specific pitches (such as middle C or *huang chung*). The actual pitches produced by the full set of twelve *lü's* have specific names (like Yellow Bell, Forest Bell, and the like).[4] When the Chinese arrange them in ascending order they look like a Western chromatic scale, but they are not; they are merely a listing of

[4] The various names attached to pitches by the Chinese may have had specific acoustical-scientific meanings. See Fritz Kuttner, "A Musicological Interpretation of the Twelve Lus in China's Traditional Tone System," *Ethnomusicology*, IX, No. 1 (Jan., 1965).

all the tonal material available for constructing five-note scales or modes within these scales. The sixth and seventh *lü* tones (F-sharp and B in Example 6-3) were called "changing" (*pien*) tones; they seem to have been used as passing tones or modal changes within a basic five-tone framework.

As implied above, the five-tone basic scale could be transposed by putting the note *kung* on any one of the twelve *lü* pitches and thence constructing a five-tone scale in the proper interval sequence. It was also possible to construct modes within each one of these transposed pentatonic scales. Chinese music theorists, like their Near Eastern and Indian counterparts, continued over the centuries to create ever more elaborate systems. The fact that the *lü* system created acoustically perfect (untempered) but musically inconvenient pitches caused other Chinese scholars to struggle with the problem of tempered tuning. Some attempts seem to date as early as the sixth century A.D., and the system later adopted in the West first appears in China in the writings of the sixteenth-century Prince Chu Tsai-yü (*c.* 1596). All these noble experiments seem to have had little effect on the actual condition of Chinese music. It remained untempered and pentatonic even though the diatonic seven-tone scale was described in the fifth-century *History of Later Han* and in T'ang period (618-907) sources, and tempered tuning was introduced in the Ch'ing (1644-1911).

It is important to keep the basic pentatonic scale in mind, for many studies list notes in larger scale-like orders, either for the sake of theoretical speculations or to illustrate extra-musical, nonscalar relationships. For example, the twelve chromatic *lü* tones have been divided into two six-tone series according to whether they are generated by going up a fifth or down a fourth (see Example 6-2). The main function of such a listing is to organize the tones of Chinese music along the lines of the male-female, *yin* and *yang* principles of Chinese metaphysics. Thus, the legends explain that the notes of the upper series are those sung by the male phoenix bird, the lower series those of the female. The influence of such symbolic structures is seen in some of the imperial panpipes (*p'ai hsiao*) in which the male and female pipes are arranged separately, outward from the middle of the instrument rather than in ascending order. *Yin* and *yang* tones also tended to be arranged separately in the racks of sixteen bronze bells (*pien chung*) and similar sets of stone chimes (*pien ch'ing*) so popular in Chou court orchestras.

The twelve tones themselves were supposedly created in order to provide a cosmologically correct *kung* tone for the proper scale to be used in each of the twelve months or the twelve hours. The five tones, in turn, were connected with the five directions, the five elements, and many other qualities in a manner that reminds us of the other great musico-philosophical constructs of Asia and the Near East.

The importance of music as a reflection of the natural philosophy and orderly penchants of Chinese thought has been much emphasized in the writings on ancient Chinese music. However, this plethora of legendary analogies has combined with the pictographic nature of the Chinese language to cloud the fact that the ancient Chinese were skilled, knowledgeable acousticians. Many of the fanciful legends and terms are actually ancient ways of reporting important scientific and musical findings derived from controlled, empirical experiments. At least two thousand years ago, Chinese scientists knew as much about soundproof research laboratories, the laws of vibrations, and tuning as did Western scientists at the turn of the present century.

Like the Greek theoretical foundations of Western music, many of the early Chinese concepts concerning music have faded away, while others remain as the subliminal heritage of modern musicians. Besides the whole-step pentatonic scale, many of the structural principles of Chinese music today can be traced to the grand syntheses created in an age that parallels the era of Aristotle and Pythagoras but predates Al Farabi or Pope Gregory by several centuries. Thanks to the literacy of Chinese and Greek civilizations, we can still savour some of the wonders of the ancient theoretical foundations of music, though the concomitant practical musics of both the East and West are lost. However, there are descriptions of musical instruments which, in China, give us tantalizing hints of the flavor of a musical cuisine as exotic as even the most romantic Westerner could imagine.

The Chinese genius for orderly systems appears again when we study musical instruments. These were classified under the so-called "eight sounds" (*pa yin*) system, which differentiated instruments by the main material from which they were made—earth (pottery), stone, metal, skin, wood, bamboo, gourds, and silk. This system often relates to the design of the Chinese characters used to write the names of Chinese instruments. For example, the character for the clay ocarina (*hsuan* 壎) has the symbol for earth at the left; the stone chime's character (*ch'ing* 磬) has the stone symbol on the bottom; and the idiogram for metal appears in the word for the bronze bells so often seen in books on Chou dynasty art.

The ancient lists contain wonderful legends about instruments as well as much accurate information. For example, the same Huang-ti who "ordered" the invention of music is said to have had a drum made from the skin of a one-legged monster which, when struck with a huge bone, could be heard for hundreds of miles. This fabulous drum is listed under the "skin" category along with several types of drum that actually existed in ancient times. An exotic entry in the "wood" category—and an instrument that does in fact exist—is the *yü*, a model of a crouching tiger with a serrated ridge or a set of wooden slats along its backbone. A split bamboo whisk was swept along its back to indicate the end of a piece in

Confucian ritual music. It is still used that way in Korea, as is an ancient wooden box (*chu*), which is thumped with a pole stuck through a hole in the top.

Under the "bamboo" category one finds the *lü* pipes bound together as a panpipe (*p'ai hsiao*). Both the vertical notched *hsiao* flute and the horizontal *ti* flute are in this category. The *sheng* mouth organ (Plate XII, figure 37), although using seventeen bamboo pipes, is classified as a gourd instrument because of the gourd-like wind chest in which the pipes are set. We have explained earlier how on the Southeast Asian relatives of this instrument chords may be played by closing the hole on the side of each pipe, thus activating the free reed that is placed at the windchest end of each pipe. The *sheng* uses the same system, though the pipes are much shorter (compare figure 32 and figure 37). The placement of the pipes in a circle around the edge of the wind chest facilitates the performance of chords as well as melodies. The ancients say that the *sheng* sound is an imitation of the cry of the phoenix bird and that its shape is that of a phoenix with folded wings. The facts of history say that it is the oldest known organ principle in the world and was apparently responsible for the introduction of the reed organ into Europe in the seventeenth century. We shall meet it again in modern Chinese music and in the court ensemble of Japan.

The "silk" category contains a surprisingly large number of multiple-stringed zithers[5] with movable bridges, such as the twenty-five-stringed *se* and the thirteen-stringed *cheng*. The most famous of the "silk" instruments, however, is the seven-stringed *ch'in* (Plate XII, figure 35). This instrument and its music have long been associated with Confucius and the life of the intellectual in China. A look through any collection of Chinese landscape paintings as they survive from later periods will inevitably reveal a bearded scholar either seated behind his *ch'in* while viewing the scene or followed by an apprentice carrying this lovely instrument. Unlike the other zithers of China, the *ch'in* has no bridges. Rather it is played by touching the strings along and between thirteen positions marked with inlaid ivory dots on the side of the instrument. Although the *ch'in* is played in this divisive manner, its seven strings are tuned according to the cyclic principles (C, D, E, G, A, c, d). Some scholars claim that the many sliding effects, harmonics, and other special strokes used by both hands were derived in the international period from the *gamaka* ornamentations of India.

While no *ch'in* music survives from Confucian times, the notation used during the Sung dynasty (960-1279) shows a system of symbols that look like Chinese characters but actually are artificial constructs that indicate simultaneously the note, the fingering, and the stroke to be used.

---

[5] Compare this with the emphasis on harps and dulcimers in the ancient Near East.

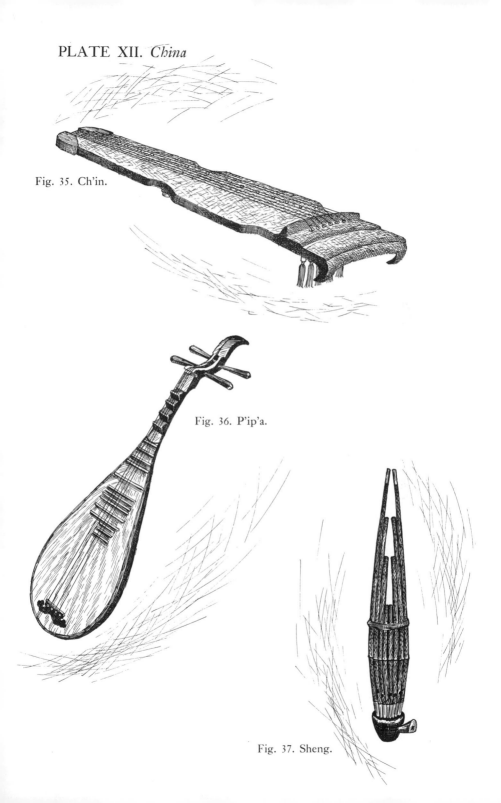

PLATE XII. *China*

Fig. 35. Ch'in.

Fig. 36. P'ip'a.

Fig. 37. Sheng.

Since the classics were written by scholars in Confucian oriented courts, they do not give a complete picture of the musical life of ancient China. For example, outside of the few folk festivals mentioned above, the music of the peasants was unnoticed, though it is said that many ancient poems were court versions of folk songs. Nevertheless, by at least the third century B.C. the basic categories of court music were codified. The two principal divisions were ritual music (*ya yueh*) and banquet music (*yen yueh*). Within the Confucian ritual were found six dances, divided into military (*wu wu*) and civil (*wen wu*) forms. Over the centuries the precise meanings and contents of common and court music, ritual and banquet music, and the civil and military dances changed, but the distinctions themselves survived until the twentieth century. We shall see them first during their systemization under the Han dynasty (202 B.C.-120 A.D.).

Because of the destruction of many books and instruments under Ch'in-shih-huang-ti in the short Ch'in dynasty (221-206 B.C.), the court music of the Chou period disappeared, but the idea of court music was far from dead in the great intellectual revival under the Han ruler, Wu-ti (140-87 B.C.). A governmental office of music (*yueh fu*) was established whose job it was to set the correct pitch of the *lü's*, supervise all ceremonies, and also collect regional popular and folk music as well as poetry for court songs. The basic *lü* pipe preserved in this office was also used as a standard measure for length and weight. Thus, the music office was a bureau of the Office of Weights and Measurements and remained so through many dynasties even though, in the later Han period, bronze bells were used as a standard for pitch in place of the *lü's*.

The orchestras used in the Han official court rituals and banquets were quite large and, somewhat like Western symphony orchestras, consisted of large numbers of string and wind players plus a backing of percussionists. (The instruments, of course, were of the types mentioned earlier; thus their sound was totally different from their modern Western counterparts.) The ritual dance troupe was also generally large. In both cases the number of participants was governed by Confucian numerology.[6]

Non-Confucian musics were found in certain warrior dances (not the *wu wu* mentioned above), whose accompaniment relied heavily on stone and metal instruments, and in the banquet music of the women's quarters. In the latter the sound of strings and winds prevailed. The ladies sang songs based on folk texts to create a light-hearted mood. Theatricals had already been known in the Chou dynasty and continued to find a place in

---

[6] Peter Crossley-Holland has pointed out that the number of tiles in the floor of the Temple of Heaven in Peking matches the number of linear measuring units used to construct the basic *lü* pipes. Such is the thoroughness of Confucian numerology. See "Chinese Music" in *Grove's Dictionary of Music* (1954), II, 228.

the court, though the great flourishing of Chinese drama was centuries ahead.

By the end of the Han period, the Chinese Empire had reached its maximum size and surpassed its contemporary giant, the Roman Empire, in territory, population, and power. As the Chinese armies and the foreign traders returned from Central Asia and Northern India, they brought with them many exotic items, including "barbarian" instruments such as a crooked-neck relative of the *p'ip'a* lute (Plate XI, figure 36) around the second century B.C. and, in the first century A.D., a new religion, Buddhism. When the Han dynasty began to break up and the barbarians themselves invaded the borderlands of China with renewed vigor, the effects of this new religion and the new musics began to change the surface of Chinese music. It was the Six Dynasties period (222-589 A.D.) that saw the struggle of the old ways against an ever-increasing influx of new ideas. In music, as in many other basic Chinese attitudes, the foundations laid in the more insular formative period remained essentially the same during the international period that followed.

The International Period (fifth century through tenth century). The two major areas of cultural and political vulnerability in China were its western and northern borders. During the Six Dynasties period the Chinese heartland was no longer unified; hence we find that the North China kingdoms were heavily influenced by music from both border areas, while the southern kingdoms held as best they could to the old court and popular traditions—though they also were affected by the flood of new ideas coming over the Western trade routes. The influences from the North consisted primarily of militaristic drum, trumpet, and oboe music; including Tartar cavalry bands. The Western influences included Indian music theory, particularly as it related to Buddhist chanting. The main streams of Western music came from the Central Asian Gandharan, Iranian, and Tokharian cultures. These traditions came into China by three main routes: via the trade cities of Khotan to the south (third to fifth centuries), Kucha in the center (fourth through eighth century), and Turfan to the north (fifth through ninth centuries). Though all these towns are now only dust mounds in the deserts, their artifacts and cave paintings, along with the larger Buddhist cave paintings in China proper, reveal a host of new instruments including cymbals, the Assyrian angle harp (*k'ung hou*), and a variety of plucked lutes, some of which have been traced back as far as ancient Egypt.[7]

It was the short Sui dynasty (589-618) that began to reunify China. In the process, court music was revived, this time with many of the new instruments added or with entirely new music ensembles imported from

[7] The most persistent claimant for an Egyptian origin is Professor Hisao Tanabe, whose writings in Japanese present the theory in detail. West-to-East musical migrations are seen in Shigeo Kishibe's "The Origin of the P'ip'a," *Transactions of the Asiatic Society of Japan*, Second series, XIX (1940), 259-304.

outside China. All these national musics were organized by the government into seven and later nine kinds of music. The codification and flourishing of international music in China, however, occurred in the brilliant T'ang dynasty (618-907) which followed.

Some idea of the international scope of the T'ang musical world can be seen in a breakdown of the ten kinds of music (*shih pu chi*) found in the government music bureau at the time of the famous ruler Hsuan-tsung (712-756). The most distant musics were a band of five instruments from Samarkand, beyond the Pamir mountains, and another group from Bokhara still farther west of that. Kashgar, at the doorway of the Western world, sent yet another music. The trade centers of Kucha and Turfan each had orchestras at the court (Khotan by this time was destroyed). A sixth music came from India to the southwest, while another came from Korea to the northeast. One group of musicians specialized in a music that combined Chinese and Kucha styles. Indigenous Chinese folk music from earlier periods was yet another category, and finally, a large orchestra using twenty-five different kinds of instruments was dedicated to performing Chinese court music. In addition to the ten official kinds of music, there are records of musical tribute coming from Tibet and the kingdoms of Southeast Asia. Each of these groups maintained its own repertoire, instruments, performers, and dancers. Even the color of their costumes varied. Truly this was an international period, and the fads for various "western" musics and manners that ran through the populace were the subject of many essays and reproving poems by classical scholars of the time.

This host of foreign and native musicians resided primarily in the capital city of Ch'ang-an, supported out of tax funds as government slaves. But even slavery had its ranks, and many musicians rose to comfortable positions by way of their musical or political talents. In addition, there were a great many musicians and dancers dedicated to purely secular entertainment. In the days of Hsuan-tsung, the section of Ch'ang-an called the Pear Garden (*Li Yüan*) was a huge school for the training of such personnel. Its music was a synthesis of foreign and Chinese secular styles, and it is said that the emperor himself taught there.

Since the days of Kao-tsu (618-626), selected girls (*kung nü*) had been taught music in a special school inside the court (the *nei chiao fang*). One of the earliest extant pictures of Chinese secular music shows a group of these ladies entertaining the emperor.[8] In another school outside the court (the *wai chiao fang*), professional female musicians were trained; these became a source for the teahouse girls in the later T'ang dynasty and are distant ancestors of the famous Japanese geisha.

To the basic distinction between court music (*ya yüeh*) and common

[8] See Shigeo Kishibe, "A Chinese Painting of the T'ang Court Women's Orchestra" in *The Commonwealth of Music* (New York: Free Press of Glencoe, Inc., 1965), pp. 104-17.

music (*su yueh*) of previous eras, the T'ang dynasty added the category of foreign music (*hu yueh*). While we can see each of these as a separate style in some of the musics listed above, the important characteristic of the period was the manner in which the three musics exchanged idioms and instruments. This adventuresome spirit resulted in new instruments as well, such as a set of sixteen iron slabs (*fang hsiang*) used in imitation of the bell and stone chime-sets of before. The greatest changes instrumentally, however, came in the chordophones.

We have mentioned the appearance of harps and plucked lutes. The former are the only harps to play any significant role in Chinese music. Among the lutes, the *dram-snyan*—still used in Tibet (see Example 6-1)— is of interest not only because it is mentioned in T'ang documents but also because it may have led to the better-known three-stringed lute tradition of later Chinese and Japanese times (see figure 39 and figure 45). The four-stringed, pear-shaped *p'ip'a* (Plate XII, figure 36) was the dominant lute of T'ang times and was used extensively in ensembles. It also had a repertoire of descriptive solo pieces and was used to accompany songs. In T'ang times we begin to learn the names of pieces, the composers, and the events for which given pieces were written. In the repertoire of the court ritual music, for example, there are titles and descriptions of eight pieces played without strings as "standing music," probably outside in the courtyard, and six pieces played as "sitting music" inside the palace halls. Famous emperors and empresses are credited with the composition of such hit pieces as "The Lion Dance of the Five Directions" or "The Battleline Smashing Music." The choreography of the dances required from four to one hundred and eighty dancers. The larger groups sometimes formed letters in a manner familiar to viewers of American football half-time extravaganzas.

A few T'ang documents give general descriptions of the manner in which pieces were performed. However, useful detail about performance practice is lacking except as it is implied by the imitations of T'ang music found in the surviving court orchestras of Korea and Japan. There have been attempts in China to revive certain T'ang popular melodies[9] primarily as they appear in collections of later dynasties. At present the closest we can come to the spirit of such T'ang dance pieces as "A Night of Flowers and Moonlight by the Spring River" is to read the poetry of Li Po or gaze at T'ang clay figurines with their flying sleeves, curved bodies, and aristocratic heads encased in *haute coiffure*.

Since the huge and complicated art-music establishment of the T'ang period was supported by tax funds, it declined rapidly as soon as the imperial fortunes began to wane. The singing girls of the court (*chi nü*)

[9] One document of T'ang melodies has survived and has been transcribed, though its lack of rhythm and orchestration tell us little about how it was performed. See Laurence Picken, "Twelve Ritual Melodies from the T'ang Dynasty," in *Studia Memoriae Béla Bartók Sacra* (London: Boosey & Hawkes, 1959), pp. 145-71.

became teahouse singing girls (*chi kuan*), while male musicians from the court found themselves at liberty to starve or to find new audiences. Theatres and brothels, both of which had always been present in some form in China, began to absorb more of the governmental musicians and dancers, and the center of Chinese musical interest shifted from Confucian rites and courtly life to the demands of the public stage or the homes of wealthy merchants.

During the chaotic Five Dynasties and Ten Kingdoms period (907-979), a few more "barbarian" instruments such as the two-stringed Mongolian fiddle (*hu ch'in*, Plate XIII, figure 38) were adopted in China, but this time such additions are first noted in the theatre rather than in the court. China had passed its peak as a land of cosmopolitan taste and as a pace-setter for the Asian world. However, out of the new Chinese society came the standard practices of a national style that are still in effect today.

The National Period (tenth through nineteenth centuries). The Sung dynasty (960-1279) brought a new stability and prosperity to China based primarily on military and mercantile activity. The court periodically refurbished Confucian music, though its main musical contributions came through new theoretical studies and indirectly through the support of huge encyclopedic and historical compilations and the fostering of new poetry forms. The latter developed along two lines, each of which reflected important factors in the further development of Chinese music. One form was chanted in such a way as to exploit the basic tone levels of the Chinese language. This form was called *shih*, a term applied to many earlier poetry styles as well as to this late T'ang and early Sung development. Some feel that the relation of speech tones to melodic structure has been fundamental to Chinese music since at least this era.[10] The other form of poetry, *tz'u*, also uses the tone system, but it originated in songs sung in the entertainment districts of the cities and reflected a new emphasis on urban secular music. The freer meters and colloquial language of the *tz'u* were important factors in the theatrical music that was soon to dominate the Chinese scene. The use of standard melodies for the singing of different poems in both the *shih* and *tz'u* traditions also became idiomatic of Chinese vocal music, particularly as it appeared in drama.

Sung dynasty writers distinguished between two kinds of drama, the southern (*nan ch'ü*) and northern (*pei ch'ü*) styles. Though both used the *tz'u* poetical forms, the southern school favored the pentatonic scale and emphasized flute accompaniment, while the North used a seven-tone scale and the *p'ip'a*. In addition to these two kinds of theaters, there was a variety of street and restaurant entertainments and lute-accompanied story tellers. In all, the Sung cities were as lusty and gay as eighteenth-century London.

[10] See John Levis, *Foundations of Chinese Musical Art* (New York: Paragon, 1963); a reprint of the original 1936 publication.

When the Mongols under Jenghiz Khan, and later Kublai Khan, put an end to Sung glories, they by no means stopped the growth of Chinese opera. The infusion of Mongol lutes and percussion instruments, in fact, was an important contribution to opera in the succeeding Yüan dynasty (1279-1368). Yüan drama (*Yüan ch'ü*) continued the distinction of northern (*tsa ch'ü*) and southern (*hsi wen*) styles. The stereotyped melodies of previous poetical forms now became the *ch'ü p'ai*, tunes with specific emotional or situational connotations which operated as repertory-wide clues to the meaning of aria texts. They were somewhat like the *Affektenlehre* of the European baroque or the leitmotives of Wagner. The acrobats and pantomimists of the street found their place within the opera, with a concomitant brightening of the productions.

While the emphasis of this period was on vocal music, instrumental forms existed as well. For example, the *p'ip'a* lute and *ch'in* zither, though used for vocal accompaniment, developed extensive solo repertoires. During the Sung dynasty, manuscripts and the first printed music included instrumental pieces, some of which claimed to have been copied from T'ang sources. Many collections survive from the succeeding Ming dynasty (1368-1628). The composite form of *ch'in* notation used in these works has already been discussed (see page 112). Other instrumental notations used a symbol for each note in a five- or seven-note scale and named, at the start of the piece, the type of scale and mode desired. Tempo and meter markings also appeared, but rhythmic details for the individual melodies were lacking, causing a variety of interpretations over the centuries. Nevertheless, the two basic types of instrumental solo music found in Sung and Ming times have remained dominant to the present day. The first type is the descriptive or impressionistic piece. The *p'ip'a* is particularly famous for its battle pieces, in which the clash of armor, singing of arrows, and cries of the wounded are all depicted; the *ch'in* tends more towards impressionistic scenes like "The Drunken Fisherman." The second type of solo instrumental music is the abstract piece, best known in a kind of variation form used by the *ch'in*. The social context of instrumental music was still the court, but the moneyed merchant could also enjoy this music. This led to the Ming and Ch'ing (1644-1911) periods to a kind of bourgeois chamber music using the *p'ip'a* plus newer theatre instruments such as the two-stringed fiddles (the *erh hu* and *hu ch'in*, figure 38), the three stringed plucked lute (*san hsien*, figure 39), and the "moon" guitar (*yueh ch'in*, figure 40) with four strings in double courses. Flutes included the end-blown *hsiao*, with four finger holes on top and one on the back, and the side-blown *ti*, with six finger holes. The latter is noted for its three extraneous holes. Two holes at the end of the instrument are used to tie a long silk tassle, which adds a decorative touch to the performance; the other, just below the mouth hole, is covered with thin rice paper, which adds a gentle buzzing quality to the instrument's tone. Some of the chamber music using these various instruments is purely instrumental, while

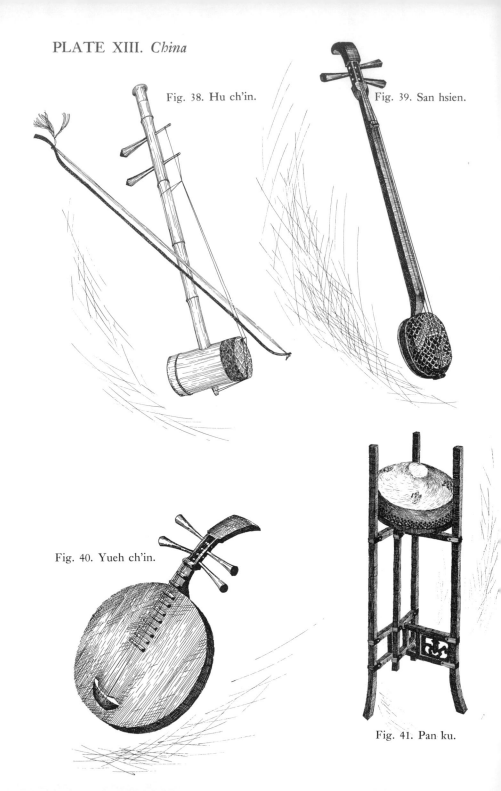

PLATE XIII. *China*

Fig. 38. Hu ch'in.

Fig. 39. San hsien.

Fig. 40. Yueh ch'in.

Fig. 41. Pan ku.

other pieces have a vocal part. In either case, much of the chamber music repertoire is derived from the all-pervading style of Chinese opera.

The generic term for Chinese opera is *hsi ch'ü*. A survey of its history since the fading of Yüan drama reveals some three hundred different varieties of opera, many of which survive today. Most of these are small theatricals amounting to regional folk dramas. Others are urban professional theatres that use one of the many dialects of Chinese and are generally named after their location—for example, Canton, Fukien, Amoy, Shanghai, or Peking opera. These many operatic forms differ not only in text but also in tone systems, accompaniment, voice quality, and musical structure. Distinctions in tone systems and accompaniment have already been made in our general discussion of northern and southern styles (page 118). Distinctions in voice quality range from the famous high, nasal falsetto of Peking to the rather low, open-throated tone of Canton. The latter is matched in the Cantonese accompaniment by a preference for softer-sounding instruments. These include the *yang ch'in*, the so-called "butterfly harp"—which is not a harp at all, but a dulcimer—a Chinese version of the Near Eastern *santur*, which was imported into China in the eighteenth century.

Though Chinese opera includes instrumental music for dances, pantomimes, and interludes as well as vocal recitatives, its characteristic musical styles are found in the arias. There are two general approaches to the settings of arias in China. The first, called *lian ch'ü*, selects from a body of standard short pieces a set of works that are appropriate to the moods of a given drama. This kind of structure is possible only when the text uses a rather rigid poetical form. Hence, the *lian ch'ü* were used in the oldest opera forms, like those of the Sung dynasty around the twelfth century, and in the remnants of Ming opera found in the opera tradition called *k'un ch'ü*. The standard-piece approach is linked to the court poetry traditions mentioned earlier, though it has a basis in the structure of folk theatricals as well.

The second approach, called *ban ch'iang*, uses stereotyped melodies rather than complete pieces. These melodies are subject to extensive variation depending on the dramatic situation. Rhythm plays a very important role in determining how these tunes are used. This approach began in the Ming dynasty but prevailed most strongly during the Ch'ing (1644-1911) in a style of opera called *ban tzu ch'iang* after the wooden block (*ban tzu*) used to set the rhythm. A unique and extreme example of rhythmic emphasis is found in the *kao ch'iang* opera of Szechwan and Hunan provinces, which originally used only gongs and drums as accompaniment. Modern productions of such operas have added complete songs in the *lian ch'ü* style accompanied by winds and strings. In truth, the two basic approaches, the complete-song and the stereotyped-tune-and-rhythm methods, are both found within one style today. They are a matter of emphasis rather than exclusion. It is the mixture of these approaches, along with various features of the northern and southern styles, that makes modern opera interesting. The specific application of these principles is best seen in the dominant form today called *ching hsi* or Peking opera.

The strength of Peking opera comes from its combination of features from many regional styles. It offers a variety of sights and sounds—from deafening preludes of crashing cymbals and stages filled with sword-swinging acrobats to pathetic arias sung by a comely girl or a female impersonator standing before a set consisting of only two chairs and a cloth-covered table. In discussing its music, we will start with the orchestra.

Two basic kinds of instrumentation are used in Peking opera. The first is used for battles or military entrances and consists of a battery of gongs, cymbals, and drums, plus the double-reed *sona*, already familiar to us from the Near East and South Asia (see Plate VI, figure 18). The other ensemble is used for all civil and domestic scenes and is, therefore, heard more often. Its instrumentation varies with each number according to the mood; however, two kinds of instruments are basic, a time-beater and a bowed lute.

The most common time-beater is a *pan ku* or *tanpi ku* (Plate XIII, figure 41). It consists of a skin stretched over a set of wooden wedges bound in a circle and so hollowed out that only a small part of the skin covers a cavity at the center of the drum. The sharp, dry, cracking sound produced by this instrument penetrates nicely through the other instrumental sounds—as it should, since the *pan ku* player is the leader of the orchestra. The rhythm he plays (see Example 6-4) often determines the nature of the piece. Additional time-beaters used in conjunction with or in substitution for the *pan ku* include wooden blocks, thick wooden sticks, and various sets of wooden clappers often played in the manner of castanets. The generic term for most of the clappers is *pan* (a term using a different Chinese character from that of the *pan* in *pan ku*).

The standard bowed lute of Chinese opera is the *hu ch'in* (Plate XIII, figure 38), the barbarian fiddle borrowed from the Mongols around the time of the Yüan dynasty. Its pegs are in the back of its neck so that the two strings, tuned in fifths, are aligned vertically over the snakeskin soundboard. This position allows the bow to pass between them rather than over them in the manner of Near Eastern bowed lutes. The *hu ch'in* is played with the finger along the string like the *rebab*, rather than pressed against the finger board like the Western violin. The *hu ch'in* leads the ensemble in performing the stereotyped melodies as set in the matrix of the time beaters. It is often doubled by a larger, two-stringed *erh hu* fiddle, which plays an octave lower and is similar to the *hu ch'in* in appearance, except that its body may be either hexagonal or round. There is also a four-stringed *hu hu* fiddle that may appear.

The plucked lutes most commonly found in opera orchestras are the *p'ip'a* (figure 36) the *yueh ch'in* (figure 40), and the *san hsien* (figure 39). The *yueh ch'in* has a thin metal plate suspended inside its wooden body to add resonance. A similar metal strip is suspended inside the neck of the larger northern form of the *san hsien*, although this is not found in the smaller southern form. Either form may appear in the opera.

The only melodic aerophone in the opera civil orchestra is the *ti tzu* flute mentioned earlier. It was the only accompaniment used for the old *k'un ch'ü* style and still can be heard occasionally in a solo or duet backing for an aria. Normally, like all the other melodic instruments listed so far, it plays a heterophonic version of the main melody. The *sheng* mouth organ can also be used melodically in opera, though it usually adds harmony in fourths or fifths.

Various sizes of cymbals (*po*) and thin knobless gongs (*lo*) show up in the civil orchestra as well as in the military one. Their most important use is in the long percussion overtures that begin most scenes, and as accompaniment for recitatives. At the end of each phrase in a recitative, the time-beater will lead in a short clash of cymbals and gongs. These sounds are functionally rather like the chords plunked on the harpsichord in eighteenth-century Western opera recitatives.

The voice quality and range used in a Peking opera depend on the character portrayed. Heroes use a throat-ripping rasp, while heroines use a high, thin tone derived from the stylizations of the female impersonators who dominated the feminine roles until recent times. All the vocal styles, like those of Western opera, are artificial; that is, they are the result of deliberate training. They require years of rigorous practice and, when brought to perfection, they are capable of portraying a wide range of emotions. In this they are aided by the specific connotations of the stereotyped melodies they perform.

While there are several distinct types of tunes in Peking opera, most melodies are classified as either *hsi p'i* or *erh huang*. Chinese writers say that these two melody types are varied by being played in different rhythms as regulated by the time-beaters. Though often spoken of as specific melodies, the two categories are really prototypes of various tunes chosen according to the needs of a given dramaturgical situation. Even when the same melody is performed, it is highly varied by the individual artist in each situation.[11]

Examples 6-4*a* and *b* illustrate some of the ways in which the singer and the orchestra handle arias. Both instrumental introductions are of the *hsi p'i* type. Example *a* is marked as *hsi p'i yüan pan*, which means that the basic meter is one drum and one beat on a beater. Note that the actual rhythm played is quite varied—just as one can play many rhythms within the framework of a given time signature in Western music. Example *b* is

[11] An excellent way to see how great the variation in a melody can be is to look at the eleven different versions of the same passage, as sung by the same singer at different times, in the book by Liu T'ien-hua entitled *Selections from the Repertoire of Operatic and Terpsichorean Melodies of Mei Lan-fang* (Peiping, 1929).

marked *hsi p'i yao pan*, which indicates that it is in a fast tempo. Both
introductions identify the mood of the piece that follows.

The main melody appears with the entrance of the singer. If one com-
pares the transcriptions of both vocal and instrumental parts, it is obvious
that the simultaneous variations of both parts create a true example of

EXAMPLE 6-4. Two Peking opera aria excerpts transcribed from the recording,
The Ruse of the Empty City (New York: Folkways Record FW 8882), side 2,
bands 1 and 6. By permission of Folkways Records and Service Corporation.

Cymbals

EXAMPLE 6–4. *Continued*

heterophony, though the voice sings in characteristic short phrases while the instruments never stop their accompaniment. In Example 6-4*b* the instrumental line is so florid that the two lines become almost independent. They are soon brought to order by a cadence climaxed with crashing cymbals. Note how the rhythm of the *pan* signals the beginning of this cadence (as it does for the one shown in Example *a*). Note also how the *pien* tone (A in our notation) is added to the pentatonic core of the melody.

The preceding two short examples can give us only an inkling of the organization of Peking opera music. Much study remains to be done, but we know enough to recognize the musical and theatrical validity of this tradition. The use of connotative melodies is of great importance in the appreciation of a given situation; and the use of rhythm to demarcate melodies and give them a sense of progression is as valid here as it was, in different forms, in the colotomic structure of the Indonesian *gamelan* and the *tala* of India. When you add to this gorgeous costumes and a troupe of acrobats, you have good theatre by any standard. It is my contention that it is also good music.

The Chinese narrative tradition does not always require such an elaborate setting. In addition to many kinds of small theatricals, there is a lovely shadow puppet tradition that uses a small ensemble of opera instruments backstage to accompany the narrator-manipulator. There are also at least two major traditions of solo narrators. The first, sometimes called *tan tz'u*, is by one performer who plays the *p'ip'a* in a steady flow of melody against which short melodic phrases are used as in the opera arias mentioned above. These pieces are usually strophic. The other narrative tradition is called *ta ku tz'u* after a small flat drum that is usually used as accompaniment. The singer often plays a castanet with his left hand and the drum with his right. A *san hsien* player may also accompany him in his strophic songs. While both these traditions have their professional performers, musical storytelling as such has belonged since at least the Sung dynasty to the itinerant street musicians whose appeal was to the peasant and the passerby. The role of both the singer and his audience has changed in the contemporary scene we have chosen to designate as the period of world music.

The World Music Period (1911–   )

In 1911, the last of the Chinese dynasties fell and a republic was declared. The stormy years that followed witnessed sporadic attempts at Westernization that were complicated by internal strife and external pressure. Western music, which had appeared in China as early as the Ming period, still found little favor with the general public, but the Chinese elite accepted it along with suits and automobiles as symbols of Western culture. Western music teachers began to appear in the cities of China, and Chinese students went to the Western conservatories. Orchestras were formed, musicales were given, and talk of a synthesis of Chinese and Western music was heard. One should mention also that European musicians in turn began to search the black notes of the piano for the mysteries of Oriental music!

The search for a new art was not particularly successful in either world. On the peasant level in China, however, a new tradition of unison singing arose as greater numbers of Chinese became involved in civil construction, civil wars, and the struggle against the Japanese. The subject matter of this music was topical and polemical, and at least one song has earned fame as the national anthem of modern China. Even in this case, the text was changed according to the "owner" of China.

Since 1949, the Communist party has held the Chinese mainland; as a result, Chinese music has been organized along the lines of Marxist-Leninist Socialism. Under this concept, as explained by the Chinese Communist leader Mao Tse-tung,[12] the function of the arts is to serve the whole mass of the nation's people (in China that means one third of the world's population) and to reflect the class struggle as well as the triumphs of Socialism. In Chinese Western-style music this has meant the creation of commemorative pictorial pieces such as "The Sacred War Symphony," an opera "The Red Guards of Hung Lake," or "The Ming Tombs Reservoir Cantata." In addition, the socialist interest in reaching the masses has forced Western-style composers to rely heavily on regional folk materials for the tunes of their works. Thus, a mainland Chinese vocal recital may include such pieces as a Tibetan "folk song" with the unlikely title of "Gifts for Chairman Mao."

The unison singing movement of the 1930's has changed into full choral singing of new compositions like "Socialism Is Good," of opera excerpts like "Looking Forward to the Liberation of the Working People All Over the World," or of choral arrangements of new folk songs such as "I'm so Happy on the Collective Farm."[13]

In attempting to mix the many regional folk styles of China with foreign choral singing and Socialist texts, individual composers have managed on occasion to create novel effects. For example, one composer adapted the swooping, heightened-speech style of a certain area in Southwest China to a female chorus piece with very original results. It is an open question whether such innovations can ever be developed beyond the experimental stage in a music that is required to communicate immediately to a theoretically classless society.

The most successful experiments in China have been in instrumental music. In keeping with the Communist interest in folk traditions and the Socialist communal spirit, various national ensembles have been formed. These often consist of regional instruments whose art is best heard in solo performance. When regional folk songs are played by ensembles of such instruments, they have a strong tendency to sound like Russian choral works or music by Rimsky-Korsakov. However, when composers use the

---

[12] See Mao Tse-tung, *On Literature and the Arts* (Peking: Foreign Language Press, 1960).

[13] The titles listed above are from printed record catalogues and music collections of about 1962.

opera orchestra as the backing for a *sheng* mouth organ or a *ti tze* flute concerto, some genuinely interesting music can be produced.

Both mainland and Formosan Chinese have shown an active interest in furthering a native Chinese tradition in the light of the idioms of world music. The emphasis on ensembles, often including Western instruments, has allowed tempered tuning to make strong inroads into Chinese idioms. The traditional arts of opera and solo instrumental music are still patronized in both Chinas, and Confucian rituals are occasionally revived on Formosa—with tennis-shoed school boys as dancers. In China as elsewhere, forms of popular and film music have appeared which combine four-squared strophic forms and international social dance rhythms with singers using hybrid vocal qualities and a mixed orchestra playing harmonized accompaniments.

Some say that Chinese music will never return to its former greatness until its theoretical-philosophical base is restored. The same has been said, of course, of Western music. It seems unlikely that the *lü's* and their cosmological significance will ever return to China, any more than the ethical power of the ancient Greek modes will ever affect the European scene again. Nevertheless, the overwhelming past and brilliant present of Chinese traditional music provide ample material for an appreciation of the musical genius of the Chinese people. Their impact on world music has been strong; and it is still evident in our last remaining area of study, the music of Manchuria, Korea, and the Asian Islands.

Bibliography and discography

References to Tibetan music are scattered, but the music itself can be heard on the Folkways record *Songs and Music of Tibet* (FE 4486) and the Contrepoint release *Musique tibétaine du Sikkim* (MC 20.119). Ernst Emshiemer's *The Music of the Mongols*, Publication 20 (Vol. VIII, part 4) of *The Sino-Swedish Expedition*, Sven Hedin, director (Stockholm: Thule, 1943) is the only extensive work dealing with that area. Further transcriptions are found in *Dix-huit Chants et poèmes mongoles*, First series, Vol. IV, of the *Bibliothèque Musicale du Musée Guimet* (Paris: Geuthner, 1937). At this writing the only commercial recording of Mongolian songs in the West is one band on the Le Chant du Monde record *Mongolie Sin-Kiang* (LDY 4039). The article "Chinese Music" in *Grove's Dictionary of Music* (1954), Vol. II, page 228, and Fritz Kuttner's "The Music of China," in *Ethnomusicology*, Vol. VIII, No. 2 (May, 1964) are excellent starting points for an understanding of Chinese music. J. A. Van Aalst's *Chinese Music* (1884) has recently been reprinted by Paragon Book Store in New York. R. H. Van Gulik's *The Lore of the Chinese Lute* (Tokyo: Sophia University, 1940) is a classic combination of scholarship and evocative writing, as is Edward Schafer's *The Golden Peaches of Samarkand* (Berkeley: University of California Press, 1963), which details the flow of exotica into T'ang dynasty China. Shigeo Kishibe's "On the Origin of the P'ip'a," in *The Transactions of the Asiatic Society of Japan*, Second series, Vol. XIX (Dec., 1940), follows the movement of one instrument from West to East. Kishibe's most significant studies of T'ang music are in Japanese.

Chinese instrumental music is nicely covered by a series of Lyrichord releases, *Chinese Classical Masterpieces for the Pipa and Chin* (LL 82), *China's Instrumental Heritage* (LL 92), *Chinese Drums and Gongs* (LL 102), *Shantung Music of Confucius' Homeland* (LL 112), and *Chinese Classical Music* (LL 72). Peking opera is heard on two folkways records, *The Ruse of the Empty City* (FW 8882) and *Beating the Dragon Robe* (FW 8883). Bruno records are best for searching out Communist-reconstructed music, for example, *China Today* (50115). Popular music is heard on the Capitol record *China* (T 10087).

7

Northeast Asia
and the Island Countries

Manchuria and Korea

We noted in the last chapter the pervasive influence of China on all the areas surrounding it. Manchuria and Korea are part of this Sinicized belt, yet their cultures present very different mixtures of foreign and domestic elements.

The nomadic tribes of Manchuria have at various times been vassals of Chinese or Mongolian dynasties as well as the conquerors and rulers of China itself. Russian and Siberian influences have also been felt. The resulting musical culture displays features of each external area. Both Lamaistic and Chinese Buddhism exist in Manchuria, as do Mongolian- and Siberian-style shamans with their pan drums. Russian-style folk choruses, in which a rhythmically free, melismatic solo is sung over a sustained chordal background, can be heard. At the same time, Chinese puppet plays and operas are a main source of entertainment. Finally, one can find, in mid-twentieth-century Manchuria, remnants of a court orchestra playing music derived from the lost court traditions of China primarily preserved as Confucian ritual music. While the names of many of the pieces played can be found in very ancient Chinese sources as well as in the repertoire of the T'ang-dynasty-inspired orchestras remaining in Korea and Japan, the instruments used in Manchuria come from around the time of the Manchu conquest of China (1644). However, the storerooms of Jehol and other Manchurian centers of culture have produced several unique instruments of great importance in the tracing of the movement of musical ideas and materials over Asia.

While Korea was also subject to long periods of Chinese domination and Mongolian intrusion, it maintained its own kingdoms which, though based on Chinese models, contained many native elements. The basic types of surviving Korean court orchestral music reflect this. They are Confucian ritual music (*aak*), Chinese T'ang and Sung dynasty pieces (*tang-ak*), and Korean court music (*hyang-ak*). The instrumentation for each differs. The basic melodic instruments are some form of double-reed aerophone (*piri*) and a flute. The *taekeum* flute is of particular interest for its length (two feet, five inches) and a membrane-covered "buzzing hole" which produces a tone of unusual richness.

Another melodic instrument is the two-stringed bowed fiddle (*hae-keum*). It looks somewhat like a *hu ch'in* (figure 38) except that the neck is curved inward in a unique manner. Several kinds of Chinese-inspired plucked lutes and a dulcimer are also used, though the main stringed instruments of both court and city music in Korea are zithers.

The basic Korean zither is the *kayakeum* (Plate XIV, figure 42). Its twelve movable bridges allow the pitch of each string to be changed. Pushing on the strings beyond the bridge with the left hand while plucking the notes with the right hand (see figure 42) gives further tonal variety to each string. The *kayakeum* is claimed as an indigenous instrument, as is the *komungo* (figure 43). This zither has six strings, the middle three of which are stretched over a set of sixteen stationary bridges. It is played with a bamboo stick. The *a'chaing* zither is unusual in that its seven strings, set on movable bridges, are bowed rather than plucked.

The main percussion instrument in all types of Korean music is the *changko*, shown in Plate XIV, figure 44. The right-hand skin is played with a stick, the left with the hand.

We have already noted some fairly exotic instruments in Korean court music, but its greatest historical treasures are China's most ancient idiophones, the racks of sixteen tuned bells (in Korean *pyonchong*), tuned slabs of iron (*panghyang*), and stone chimes (*pyonkyong*). Only in Korea can one still hear their simple but sonorous sounds. A musical curiosity of old China survives in Korea in the form of the *o*, a crouching wooden tiger

PLATE XIV. *Korea*

Fig. 42. Kayakeum.

Fig. 44. Changko.

Fig. 43. Komungo.

with a serrated backbone over which a split bamboo whisk is scraped at the end of Confucian ritual pieces. Another Chinese survival is the *pak*, a clapper made of six slats of wood held together at one end like a folded fan. The director of the orchestra begins and ends each piece with the sound of this instrument. Globular flutes and the Chinese mouth organ are also found in Korea.

The ancient traditions of the Korean courts are presently surviving primarily through the efforts of the National Music Institute in Seoul. In attempting to restore some of the old traditions, they have been aided not only by oral tradition but also by the presence of early notation books and historical sources. The most important Korean musical document is the *Akhak kwebom*, a fifteenth–sixteenth-century compendium of instrument tunings and fingerings; theoretical tone systems; choreographic patterns and the arrangement of orchestral players; and ceremonial costumes and paraphernalia.

As performed today, Korean court music is played in a rather slow tempo, often beginning in a free rhythm. There is a very florid heterophony between the melodic instruments, except for the bells and chimes, which play very simple basic melodies devoid of rhythmic variety (since the surviving notation indicates only pitches without rhythm). It is interesting to compare the mode system in which this music is set with the companion survivals in Japan, though the two musics sound quite different. Court music is virtually unknown and unappreciated in Korea today; however, it is of the greatest historical importance, for it gives us one of the last glimpses of the musical glories of the ancient Orient.

String chamber music (*pungnyu*) and classical vocal forms (*norai*) have also been preserved from the dynastic periods of Korean history. The latter include narrative songs (*kasa*) as well as lyrical poems in long (*kagok*) and short (*sijo*) forms. Today, each syllable of the text is drawn out to such an extent that the meaning is lost without seeing the poem. A more active form is the *pansori* narrative, which is sung by a fan-carrying narrator-dancer to the accompaniment of a *changko* drum. However, the most popular and widespread of Korean narratives are found in the *japka* ballads as sung primarily by professional artists or *gishang* entertainment girls. Accompanied by the driving syncopation of a *changko* drum played in a triple rhythm, the singers produce startling effects through sudden changes in style from intense throaty renditions of low, tone-centered lines to high, throat-ripping rasps reminiscent of the scat singing of jazz. Dynamics vary, and a steel-edged tone may turn into a kind of violent vibrato seldom heard in the world's vocal tradition. Tonal systems also vary, and songs may include extended slidings and sections bordering on heightened speech. This exciting vocal art and its compelling rhythmic accompaniment are major enigmas in Korean music, for they seem closer to the Flamenco and Islamic traditions than to the surrounding Oriental styles. Perhaps further music studies would shed light on possible continuities between East and West caused by the constant moves of ancient Asian hordes. At present, all that can be said is that such Korean singing deserves special attention for its unique qualities. The transcription in Example 7-1 is only a pale reflection of its true sound.

EXAMPLE 7-1. A Korean ballad song transcribed from the recording, *Japan, The Ryukyus, Formosa and Korea* (New York: Columbia Masterworks Records KL-214), side 2, band 3, item 29. Used by permission.

Korean folk, dance, and entertainment songs use the same characteristic triple rhythms, as shown in Example 7-2. When combined with the sleeve-swinging dances of Korea, the total effect is very gay. Even the shaman music of Korea maintains this quality.

EXAMPLE 7-2. A Korean entertainment song transcribed from the recording, *Japan, The Ryukyus, Formosa and Korea* (New York: Columbia Masterworks Record KL-214), side 2, band 3, item 31. Used by permission.

Another important Korean idiom is the solo instrumental variation piece (*sanjo*). It is played on many different instruments, the *kayakeum* zither being a frequent choice. In such pieces a virtuoso player can create exciting percussive effects by snapping the strings of the *kayakeum* while flying through his wavering 12/8 melodies.

Korean music, like Korean food, is spicy and rather unoriental. One is left to wonder what it means in the matrix of general East Asiatic culture. Whatever the eventual historical answer may be, the present sound of Korean music presents an exciting nonconformity in any general profile one tries to make of East Asian music.

Formosa and the Ryukyu Islands

Within the various musical cultures of the islands off the East Asiatic shore, we can find reflections of traditions already studied as well as unique regional solutions to the standard musical problems of function and structure. On Formosa, for example, one is first struck by the predominately Chinese styles of music heard in the cities. Japanese and Western occupations of the island have also left their musical marks. Tribal traditions reminiscent of Borneo and Indonesia are more evident in the jungle. Harmonic singing, like that we noted in Oceania and Borneo, and instruments like the musical bow point to a very different world from that of the urban Sino-Japanese society. In a word, when in Chapter 2 we turned from the Philippines south and westward toward Indonesia and the African-Near Eastern world, we were arbitrarily choosing one of two cultural tracks. The other moves northward through the head-hunters of Formosa and beyond.

It is difficult to say how far one can continue to trace the influence of Oceanic and Indonesian cultures beyond Formosa. The Ryukyu or Loochoo Islands, lying between Formosa and Japan off the coast of China, seem to be the point at which the myriad cultures of Asia have their last clear confrontation.

The oldest forms of Ryukyu music are the *umui* religious chants, sung primarily by priestesses (*nuru*), and the *kwena* songs. Both are sung either unaccompanied or with a drum. Two basic styles of *umui* (or *omoro* in the Japanese pronunciation) survive. The first, apparently a courtly style, consists of variants on a single centric melody (shown in Example 7-3) sung in a slow litany fashion. The second style, used in regional shrines, retains the same sliding vocal technique and short strophic characteristics of the first, but it uses many different melodies, some of much wider range, as seen in Example 7-3. This style may begin with a nonsense syllable such as *heya*, *o*, and *e*. Either style may end in a pitchless drop reminiscent of techniques used in Oceania and the Philippines. Occasional examples in three-four time are found.

Other ancient forms can be found in the Ryukyus, but the predominant styles of today are songs and dances accompanied by the three-stringed plucked lute with a snakeskin head called the *sanshin* or *jamisen*. This instrument first appeared on Okinawa, the main island of the Ryukyu chain, in the fifteenth century. It is derived from the Chinese *san hsien* (figure 39). It is plucked with a talon-like pick attached to the right forefinger. As seen in Example 7-4, the *sanshin* plays a rather straightforward tune against which an off-beat vocal line is performed. This syncopation makes it easier to hear the words against the percussive sound of the accompaniment.

While much Ryukyuan music uses the Chinese pentatonic scale, there

EXAMPLE 7-3. Ryukyu *umui* songs transcribed from tapes accompanying Seihin Yamanouchi, *Ryukyu ocho koyo himitsukyoku no kenkyu* (Tokyo: Private edition, 1964). Used by permission.

EXAMPLE 7-4. An Okinawan song "Mo-Ashibi" transcribed from the recording, *Japan, The Ryukyus, Formosa and Korea* (New York: Columbia Masterworks Record KL-214), side 2, band 1. Used by permission.

are pieces more reminiscent of Indonesia, with their use of half steps and their rising lines. Japanese influence is seen in the use of the thirteen-stringed *koto* zither (figure 46), although many of the *koto* pieces common to both countries are played in different tone systems, the Ryukyuan versions preferring the standard pentatonic over the Japanese *yo-in* scales (see below).

Ryukyuan music is most commonly heard today as dance accompaniment. *Sanshin*, singers, and a stick drummer provide the background for dances whose hand movements often look Indonesian, costumes Chinese, and floor patterns Japanese. However, the quick-stepping feet are Okinawan, and the over-all combination is unique to Ryukyuan culture.

Japan[1]—Folk music

Japan is a country of many islands. This geographical fact has combined with a long history of feudalism to create strong regional folk traditions. Nevertheless, these traditions have certain points in common. Japanese folk song tends to be sung in a high, tight-throated, melismatic fashion. Much of it tends toward the *parlando-rubato*. Dance songs are, of course, in rhythm, usually duple. The standard dance accompaniments are hand-clapping, or barrel drums with two tacked heads played with sticks. Festival music usually uses drums and bamboo flutes, plus occasional small brass gongs. The generic term for such ensembles is *hayashi*.

Japan has many folk theatricals that appear during festivals. These include a variety of animal dances, from Chinese-inspired lions to fearsome bands of deer with large horns and bamboo "antennae" projected high in the air. Elaborate flowered hats and grotesque masks can also be seen. Many of the pantomime theatricals and ritual dances are related to the ancient theatricals of the court or to the surviving professional traditions, in which cases other instruments tend to appear.

The three-stringed plucked *shamisen* or *samisen* lute (Plate XV, figure 45) did not enter Japan before the sixteenth century and thus does not tend to be used in older theatricals. However, it is used frequently to accompany regional and occupational folk songs. As seen in Example 7-5, it sometimes plays an ostinato against the vocal line. Example 7-5 uses the *in* scale, one of the two basic Japanese forms. The other, the *yo*, is related to the standard pentatonic and is derived from earlier courtly tonal systems.

In modernized Japan, folk traditions are kept alive by local chambers of commerce, Shinto shrines, and Buddhist temples. The ability to sing or perform a folk dance has also become as much a part of a businessman's qualifications as his skill at golf or cost accounting. Thus, folk song has

---

[1] Part of the following material is drawn with the publisher's permission from *Japanese Music and Musical Instruments* and *Nagauta: The Heart of Kabuki Music* by William P. Malm (Tokyo and Rutland, Vermont: Charles E. Tuttle Co., Inc.).

EXAMPLE 7-5. A Japanese folk song, "Sado Okesa," transcribed from the record-ing, *Traditional Folk Songs of Japan* (New York: Folkways Record FE 4534), side 2 (B), band 7. By permission of Folkways Records and Service Corporation.

managed to keep a closer contact with modern life than many of the other Japanese art traditions.

Japanese art music—ancient traditions

There are two ancient foundations for Japanese art music, Buddhist chant (*shomyo*) and court orchestra music (*gagaku*). Both were originally Chinese-inspired. Buddhist chant, like the litanies of the other religions, was regulated by a large number of rules, which had been set down in books and became the theoretical bases of later secular styles. Thus, the nomenclature and tone systems of Buddhism bear the same relation to Japanese art traditions as the Catholic Gregorian chant theories do to the growth of Western musical styles.

As the Japanese imperial court flourished during the Nara period (553-794), musics and dances continued to flow into the capital from many parts of the Asian continent. At the same time, native composers began to create their own compositions. These many styles were eventu-ally organized under two basic categories of *gagaku*. The first, *togaku*, consisted of pieces of Chinese and Indian origin, while *komagaku* included Manchurian, Korean, and many of the Japanese pieces. These two styles can be distinguished by their instrumentations.

Like the Korean court orchestra, the basic *gagaku* melodic instru-ment is a short double-reed aerophone (*hichiriki*). It is joined by different side-blown flutes, depending on whether the piece is *togaku* or *komagaku*. In either case, the melodic instruments play heterophonically in a harmonic matrix provided by the seventeen-piped *sho* mouth organ, derived from the Chinese *sheng* (figure 37). A large hanging barrel drum (*gaku-daiko*) with two tacked heads, played on one side with two beaters, and a small hanging gong (*shoko*) provide a colotomic structure by marking off the music into groups of two and four measures while the leader controls the tempo by playing one of two drums. In *togaku* he uses a small barrel drum (*kakko*) with two laced heads that are struck by thin sticks. In *komagaku* he uses a larger hourglass-shaped drum (*san no tsuzumi*).

Today, stringed instruments are not used in *komagaku*, nor are they used in *togaku* when it serves as dance music. Concert *togaku*, however, uses the thirteen-stringed *koto* zither (Plate XV, figure 46) and a pear-shaped *biwa* lute similar to the one shown in figure 47. As used today, these instruments do not play the melody but rather use short stereotyped melodic phrases or arpeggios which, while influenced by the mode and the melody, function primarily colotomically through the regular intervals between their entrances.

Ancient vocal forms and ritual musics for Japan's indigenous Shinto religion are also preserved in the court. Shinto music (*kagura*) in the court uses the *hichiriki* oboe and the *sho* mouth organ, plus various special instruments including a flute and a six-stringed board zither (*wagon*), which resembles the Korean *kayakeum*.

Much of the *gagaku* repertoire has been preserved in part-books which combine mnemonics with instrument fingerings. Rhythm is indicated only by marking off the colotomic divisions (usually in four beats). Though pieces are arranged in such books according to their modes, the various pitches available from a single fingering on the main melodic instruments make it difficult to determine what the actual tune is. Originally this was no problem, since the music was first taught orally—by singing the mnemonics while beating out the rhythmic divisions—and then learned on the instrument. However, whatever the relation of modern practice may be to the original product, Japanese *gagaku* is still one of the rarest and oldest orchestral musics in the world.

We have intimated that many of the principles found in these first musics are basic to Japanese music in general. One of these is the concept of getting the maximum effect from a deliberately restricted amount of material. For example, the many techniques possible on various *gagaku* instruments are generally not all exploited. Rather, there is a concentration on only a few basic sounds in order to enhance their effectiveness. At the same time, one can observe in *gagaku* performance the Japanese principle that the instruments are to be played in a graceful manner, so that the music provides an aesthetically pleasing sight as well as sound.

Gagaku and Buddhist chanting both make use of a common Japanese principle of *elastic* or *breath rhythm*. There are, of course, many steady, *metronomic* beats in Japanese music, but one also finds sections—like the

PLATE XV. *Japan*

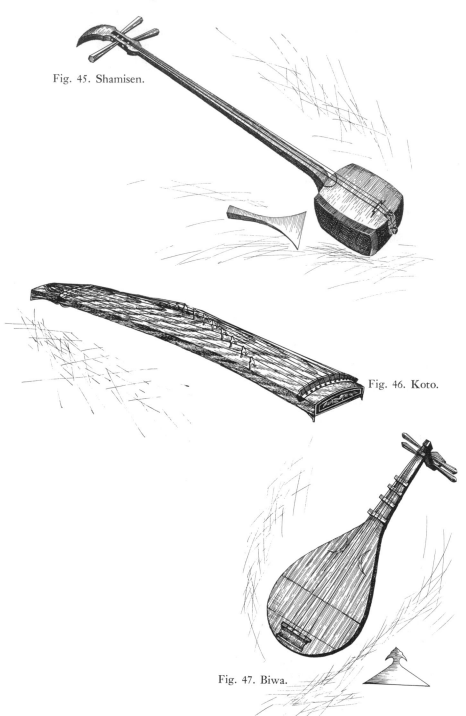

Fig. 45. Shamisen.

Fig. 46. Koto.

Fig. 47. Biwa.

opening of any *gagaku* piece—in which the beat simply cannot be con-
ducted. The melody moves from beat to beat in a rhythm more akin to
that of a breath taken in deeply, held for an instant, and then expelled. In
ensembles, such a rhythm can only be coordinated when the performers
listen and feel the music together. This is the kind of attitude we associate
with chamber music. Much Japanese music has this chamber music quality
regardless of the size of the ensemble. It also is chamber-like in the sense
that the individual instrumental lines are designed to be heard separately,
rather than merged as they are in the Western orchestra.

The string parts in *gagaku* illustrate yet another principle, the use of
stereotyped patterns. Of course, any music must have predictable patterns
if it is to be perceived in any logical manner. The manner in which such
patterns have special significances in Japanese music will become evident as we look at later theatrical traditions.

Early Japanese narrative and theatrical traditions

During the twelfth and thirteenth centuries a tradition arose called
heike-biwa, in which a famous war narration was sung to the accompaniment of a *biwa* lute (figure 47). The music consisted of lines of poetry
chanted to named stereotyped melodies separated by pitch-giving notes
or stereotyped interludes played on the lute. Many of the names of both
the vocal and instrumental patterns were derived from Buddhist chant
nomenclature. This style of narration became very popular and, though
heike-biwa itself is practically extinct today, its tradition is carried on in
a similar if more flamboyant style by modern *biwa* and *shamisen* narrators.
The *Satsuma biwa* shown in figure 47 is only one of several styles of *biwa*
used today, but the music of all tends to continue the tradition of alternating vocal and instrumental sections. In such a tradition, the notation
need only show the text plus the name of the particular pattern to be
played or sung. The individual performer must interpret these patterns
according to the requirements of the particular piece, as well as the style
of the specific guild of performers to which he belongs. This does not
mean that he improvises. In Japan there is variation but not improvisation.
Whatever be the version of a piece, it must be played as accurately as a
Mozart sonata, despite the existence of other versions of the same composition.

The many folk theatricals noted earlier, plus various courtly and
religious entertainments, contributed in the fourteenth century to the formation of Japan's first major dramatic form, the *noh*. As organized by
Kiyotsugu Kanami (1333-84) and his son, Motokiyo Zeami (1363-1443),
the *noh* made careful use of all the theatrical arts—music, dance, poetry, design, and costume. *Noh* music consists of singing, known generically as
yokyoku or *utai*, by the main actors or a unison chorus with or without

PLATE XVI. *Japan*

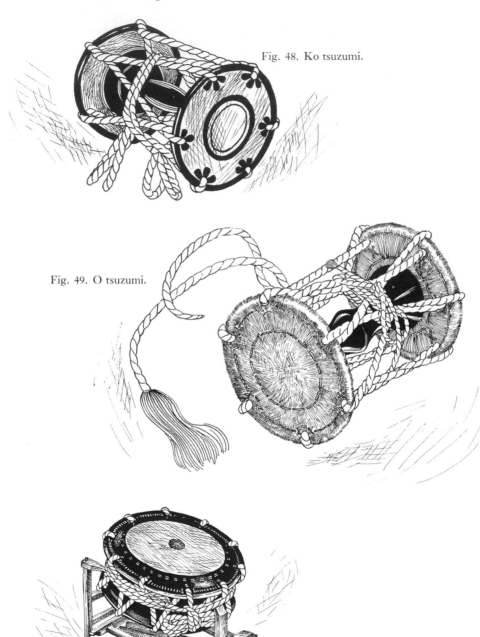

Fig. 48. Ko tsuzumi.

Fig. 49. O tsuzumi.

Fig. 50. Taiko.

the accompaniment of four instrumentalists known as the *hayashi*. The *hayashi* group also plays alone, particularly as accompaniment for dance sections. It consists of a flute (*nokan*), a shoulder drum (*ko tsuzumi*, Plate XVI, figure 48), a side drum (*o tsuzumi*, Plate XVI, figure 49), and a floor drum played with sticks (the *taiko*, Plate XVI, figure 50). The last is seldom used except in dance pieces. The flute also serves primarily for dance accompaniment, though its sound can be used to mark off sections throughout the play and to create special mood effects. However, it has no relation tonally or thematically with the vocal parts. It is the *ko* and *o tsuzumi* drums that are most intimately linked with the singing, for they provide an essential rhythmic framework into which each line of poetry must be set. As shown in Example 7-6, Japanese poetry is normally divided into seven- and five-syllable lines. In *noh* drama, these tend to be set in a framework of eight beats. Both the poetry and its framework are in turn divided into three parts: *jo*, the introduction; *ha*, the scattering; and *kyu*, the rushing toward the end. Beneath this poetry the drummers play named, stereotyped rhythmic patterns which, with the aid of various drummers' calls, help to mark the divisions of the line (the "yo" before beat three of Example 7-6 and the "ho" before beat eight).

EXAMPLE 7-6. A *noh* drama excerpt transcribed from "Hagoromo" in *Noh: Two Major Dramas* (New York: Caedmon Records TC 2019), side 2, the first entrance of the chorus. Used by permission.

Since the principle of elastic rhythm is very prevalent in *noh*, the drummers' calls are an important means of controlling and signalling the progression from one given beat to another. They have yet another function, for each named pattern has a specific set of drum calls that are an inseparable part of the pattern and are an aid in identifying it aurally. Thus, the particular arrangement of drum calls and drum sound in the pattern *mitsuji* played in Example 7-6 will never appear in quite the same manner in a pattern of some other name.

Named drum patterns are not only internally identifiable but they fall into predictable orders of progression; that is, after a given pattern is played there is a strong likelihood that another specific pattern will follow it. This kind of progression will continue until a specifically cadencing pattern appears. Similarly stereotyped patterns appear in Western music. For example, after a C major and then an F major chord, there is a strong possibility that the next chord will be G. Of course, other chords are possible—just as other rhythm patterns are possible in our Japanese example. The important point is that both systems involve sets of aurally identifiable, stereotyped patterns that tend to move in predictable succession so that the forward motion of the music is enhanced. The only significant difference between the Western and the Japanese system is that one involves vertical stereotyped sonorities called chords while the other uses horizontal rhythmic patterns. Here is one answer to the lack of harmony in much non-Western music; it is not needed, for its forward-moving function is served by a different concept of rhythm. How many times in this survey have we not seen similar "strange" uses of rhythm which thus put a third dimension into the music beyond those of melody and rhythm as they are understood in the West? The lack of the development of an involved concept of harmony in the non-West may be because its functions had already been supplanted by special uses of rhythm. The Japanese *noh* drama certainly illustrates one such use very clearly.

The *jo-ha-kyu* concept mentioned above applies to more than just a single phrase. It may be applied to large sections of a play, the entire play, or the arrangement of an entire day of plays. In a word, it is an aesthetic view of music much as the concepts of question and answer, or of arsis and thesis, are found to permeate much thinking about form in Western music. The bi-partite form is also common in Japan, but the *jo-ha-kyu* concept is the one most used by Japanese musicians when they are called upon to explain their music.

Music during Japan's Edo Period (1615-1868)

In Japan, as in the West, the major kinds of traditional music heard today arose in the period from the seventeenth through the nineteenth centuries. This time is called the Edo or Tokugawa period in Japan because the Tokugawa clan controlled the country and moved the government to a new center called Edo, known today as Tokyo. It was during this period that Japan became isolated from outside contact and thus was able to develop her own artistic resources without extensive foreign influence. It was a period marked by the rise of a merchant class and an emphasis on city life. Music reacted to the needs of this new audience.

One of the first theatricals to flourish in the new society was the puppet theatre (*bunraku*), which found its greatest audience in the business town of Osaka. The three-stringed, plucked *samisen* (in the Tokyo dialect *shamisen*, figure 45), adapted from the Ryukyuan *sanshin* in the sixteenth century, was used to accompany a singer-narrator. This music became known as *gidayu-bushi* named after its most famous singer, Gidayu Takemoto (1651-1714). It was one of many such *shamisen*-accompanied narratives, known generically as *joruri*, that flourished during the Edo period.

The musical style of *gidayu* developed from the previous *biwa* lute narratives with extensive use of stereotyped patterns and interludes. As these were connected with a theatrical art aimed at a bourgeois rather than a courtly audience, their style became more flamboyant and involved. Specific melodic phrases took on dramaturgical meaning in much the way that emotions and situations could be portrayed in Western baroque music and in Wagnerian operas through the use of special tunes. As performed today, *gidayu* music has all the melodrama and pathos of Italian opera, though a *gidayu* performer must be as great an actor as he is a singer since he speaks all the roles as well as narrates and comments on the story.

The other basic Edo Period theatrical was the *kabuki*. Traditionally an all-male theatre (though it began as all-female), *kabuki* has pleased Japanese audiences for over two hundred years with a combination of melodrama and colorful dancing. Three basic kinds of music were developed to accompany these actions, the on-stage ensemble, the narrative music, and the off-stage group.

The first on-stage (*debayashi*) ensemble in *kabuki* was the *hayashi* group of three drums and a flute mentioned earlier in connection with the *noh* drama. Next were added *shamisen*-accompanied songs derived from several genres popular in the adjacent brothel districts. Eventually the *shamisen* and singers were combined with the *hayashi* to form a new Japanese ensemble. While several different types of *shamisen* music are still played with this combination, the basic genre used today is called *nagauta* —"long songs." In keeping with the brighter spirit of *kabuki*, the drums borrowed from the *noh* developed rhythmic patterns directly related to the rhythms of the *shamisen* part. These patterns are called *chiri-kara* by the *tsuzumi* drummers (figures 48 & 49), after the mnemonic with which they are learned. However, the drummers also use *noh*-derived patterns which set up an even greater dynamic, forward progression when set against *shamisen*-vocal lines. It is common for the *taiko* drum (figure 50) and the *noh* flute to play in *noh* style while the *tsuzumi* drums support the *shamisen* line with direct rhythmic imitations. In such cases one can hear three distinct musical units: the melodic, held by the voice and *shamisen;* the rhythmic in the *tsuzumi;* and a third dynamic unit consisting of a flute and *taiko* performing many of the functions Western musicians normally associate wtih harmony. Since the *noh* flute is not operating as a melodic unit, it has no tonal or thematic relation to the *shamisen* part. In *kabuki*, the *noh* flute player may also use a folk bamboo flute if lyrical support of the melody is required. Such changes in instrumentation as well as changes in the relations of the various instrumental parts are guided by the choreography of the dance as well as by principles of form. The formal implications of changes in style and orchestration are important in such a through-composed music as *nagauta*.

The second basic *kabuki* music is the narrative (*joruri*) as derived from the *gidayu shamisen*-singer combination from the puppet tradition. *Gidayu* musicians usually sit downstage left, as they would in the puppet theatre. The various musics used in the *kabuki* often appear on stage at the same time, so that a given performance consists of interjections by two or three different groups of musicians.

The third kind of *kabuki* music is the off-stage (*geza*). The basic purpose of this music is to provide mood, set scenes, and give musical clues as to action or location. Singers, *shamisen*, flutes, drums, and a battery of special gongs and bells are used singly and in combinations. They are able to assist the drama by playing named patterns or melodies that have specific dramaturgical meaning. For example, the large *o daiko* barrel drum with two tacked heads can be made to symbolize the ocean, various degrees of rainfall, battles, or soft snowfall through the choice of the proper pattern. A given tune on the *shamisen* will indicate the weather, the time of day, or perhaps the specific location of the scene that is to follow. (Similar, less codified techniques are used in Western movie music.) In the *kabuki*, the *geza* combines with the on-stage ensembles to provide a varicolored accompaniment for one of the Orient's most enjoyable theatricals.

Not all the music of the Edo period is theatrical. In addition to many kinds of intimate *shamisen*-vocal forms, there developed other vocal instrumental traditions, such as those using the thirteen-stringed *koto* (figure 46). Movable bridges allow for several different tunings, while three picks attached to fingers of the right hand and various pressures on the strings with the left hand provide a variety of timbres and pitches. While much *koto* music is vocal, there is an important genre of variation solos (*danmono*) that are very popular. In addition, the *koto* may be combined with a singer, a *shamisen*, and a five-holed end-blown flute (*shakuhachi*) to form a chamber music (*sankyoku*) ensemble. The particularly soft sound of the *shamisen* in this ensemble is caused by the use of a heavy bridge, a thin plectrum, and strings of a special weight. Actually, each kind of *shamisen* music requires an instrument of different size as well as different accessories in order to produce a particular tone color. The *shakuhachi* also comes in various sizes; however, the choice of length is determined not by tone color but by the tuning of the other instruments in the ensemble, since Japanese music is played heterophonically. The *shakuhachi* is best heard when performing its solo literature, for a good player can produce a beautiful variety of tone colors and ornaments on this deceptively simple looking bamboo tube.

Music in modern Japan

The modernization of Japan, begun in 1868 under the Emperor Meiji, has drawn special interest from the West because of the swiftness with which it proceeded. Western music developed in Japan through two channels, the military and the educational. Originally, Western music was introduced not out of any special interest for itself, but rather from a desire to reproduce various foreign systems accurately. Thus bands were formed because they were included in the standard table of organization for military services; and music was made part of the newly formed public schools because it was included in the foreign models. Foreigners were brought to Japan as instructors, among them Luther Whiting Mason (1828-1896) who, along with Izawa Shuji (1851-1917), helped found a music teachers' college and form a curriculum for the public schools that was to affect Japanese musical life for generations. Their original intent was to combine the best of East and West, and both Western and Japanese instruments were taught at the college; similarly, song books for schools tried to include the best of the Boston public school tradition plus harmonized Japanese tunes. Unfortunately, only the Western style instrumentalists from the college went into public school teaching, the Japanese-style players returning to their own traditional world. At the same time, the children found the new military songs composed for the Chinese and Russian confrontations of greater interest than the old Japanese tunes. To capture the children's interest, many of these songs were reworked with suitable words. The net result of these various factors was that a child in school heard only Western instruments, Western children's songs, or heavily Westernized Japanese military-style music. Indeed, not until the late 1950's was Japanese traditional music to be found on music appreciation records issued for public school use. Today even the songs of Stephen Foster can be claimed as part of the Japanese musical tradition, since they have been sung by at least three generations.

Another interesting result of Japan's American-based public school music system has been that young people are trained to sing in harmonized choruses, unlike the monophonic style of traditional music. Activist groups have seized upon this training to organize workers, students, or co-religionists into choral societies which have proved very useful in recruiting new general members as well as in unifying large bodies of people for political demonstrations.

Traditional music and Western music have continued to develop in Japan on separate parallel lines. Symphonies, ballets, and operas in Western style are composed and performed with competence by Japanese artists, while *shamisen* and *koto* concerts go on apace. Attempts at synthesis have been relatively unsuccessful, since musicians on each side tend to have only a superficial knowledge of the musical principles at work on the other. As in other countries, popular music has been the most syncretic, due to its generally topical and opportunistic character. At the moment, the most obvious cross-influences in other kinds of music are the tendency to play traditional music in larger ensembles as an attempt to make it more "orchestral" and the adoption of the guild system and the obligations of the student towards his "sensei" in the teaching of Western music. Perhaps as research and education come to grips with the deeper principles of both musics there may be more significant products from the East-West encounter. At present, one can still have the best of both worlds in the music life of Japan.

The Northern Islands and beyond

On Hokkaido, Japan's most northerly island, and the Russian-occupied Shakalins beyond that, one finds the remnants of several ethnic groups quite unrelated to the general East Asiatic traditions. The best-known of these are the Ainu, a Caucasoid group with some possible racial affinity to the Australian aborigines. Their ancient narratives are sung with a quavering, half-spoken voice quality and short iterative melodies such as one may hear among the Laps of Sweden; their two- to five-stringed *tonkori* plucked zither finds few parallels outside Africa. An Ainu style of singing in which two women use each other's mouths for resonance while chanting a quick iterative refrain is similar to a game played by Canadian Eskimo children in which they pant quickly into empty oil drums. Indeed, the Ainu are a suitable close to this multicultural book, for they remind us of the continuities and varieties in the species called *homo sapiens*. If they have ancient common roots with the aboriginals with which this book began, they also have cultural relations with peoples of the Western Hemisphere beyond the Bering Sea and beyond the scope of this book.

Here we stop geographically, but the musical culture of man continues to flow across borders and continents. Nevertheless, by now the reader must know that music is not an international language. If it were, lecturers would not have to explain Beethoven to Western music lovers, nor would uninformed Western authors speak of the tuneless ditties of the savages. However, some universal principles and general patterns of musical culture seem to emerge from our survey. The need for tension and release, with all its melodic and rhythmic implications, certainly seems to be basic. The need to mark off temporal lengths of music with distinct cadence sound, the tendency to find a tonal orientation or center in melodic music, the interest in creating a sense of forward progression by melodic, harmonic, or rhythmic stereotypes, and the principle of unity along with variety are also widespread.

Among the literate societies in this survey we have found specific theoretical explanations for many tonal and compositional principles. These principles cluster around three of the four major theory systems of the modern world; the Arab-Persian, Indian, and Chinese. The fourth system, the European, has historical roots in the Greco-Roman tradition, which itself has many links with the Near Eastern synthesis. National music systems such as those of Indonesia, Uzbekistan, Japan, or the United States can be considered as satellite variations on the "big four." Of the four themselves, three based their scale structure on a divisive principle. Only the Chinese upheld a cyclic technique through the use of the *lü* pipes. The Chinese and Indian systems paid the greatest attention to the ethical and extra-musical implications of music. Such implications in the Arab-Persian system were primarily reflections of its ancient Assyrian-Egyptian base, while similar principles in the European system come out of its Greco-Roman roots. All four living traditions are closed theoretical systems; that is, they are complete in themselves and offer a thoroughly logical explanation of the particular characteristics of the music for which they were created. An appreciation of these logical but different systems is basic to an understanding of art music as a worldwide phenomenon.

Form seems to follow function in music as well as architecture, as we have seen, for example, in the various religious musics studied. The tendency to attach extra-musical values to specific instruments and elements of a tonal system is evident, particularly in the literate civilizations. More general patterns of musical distribution could be found by mapping such phenomena as the existence of harmony, the gong culture, the uses of a colotomic principle, or the presence of a given instrument such as the *rebab*. Some of these studies may give us historical information about such matters as the spread of Islam, while others may indicate more general technological or physical similarities in conditions—for instance, the prevalence of bamboo or bronze instruments.

Music is obviously as much a part of culture as a housetype or potsherd. More than some aspects of culture, however, it has the ability to be emotionally moving and aesthetically pleasing. When a carrier of a given culture becomes aware subliminally or consciously of the specific ways in which "his" music moves him through some of the principles listed above, he begins to anticipate the events of a given piece. With this anticipation comes aesthetic pleasure. On occasions we have been able to give clues as to what to listen for in a given music, so that the reader might enjoy such musical experiences as well. However, our knowledge of world music is still rather narrow, and in many cases we can offer only the exotic surfaces of non-Western music—the sensuous titillation of a recording with a strange label and curious sounds. Intellectually, our message remains the same: These sounds, whatever they seem to a given listener, are *music* to someone, and as music they contain an inner logic that can be understood and admired if one is inclined to listen to the music in its own terms. It is not necessary to enjoy the music of every land, though understanding and exposure may certainly broaden one's musical tastes. What is necessary is that one recognize the value and tolerate the existence of these many systems of music.

Hedonistically speaking, new musical pleasures may have been gained. Intellectually, many curious new facts may have been learned. These gains, however, are for naught without a new or reinforced sense of respect for man's musical inventiveness. The world is filled with logical but different systems in many other fields of human endeavor besides music. Perhaps a bit more understanding in music may contribute in a small way towards the great general need for better communication in other areas of international contact.

Bibliography and discography

Little is available in Western languages on Manchurian and Korean music. Volume 2, number 9 of the *Korea Journal* (Sept., 1962) is devoted entirely to music. Professor Lee Hye-ku, a leading native scholar, has produced a short pamphlet in English entitled *Korean Classical Music Instruments* (Seoul: The Korea Information Service, n.d.), but his major research writings are in Korean or Japanese. Seihin Yamanouchi's several volumes on Ryukyu music are in Japanese, but Jan LaRue has published two articles in English on the subject, "Native Music on Okinawa," *The Musical Quarterly*, XXXII (1946), and "The Okinawan Notation System," *Journal of the American Musicological Society*, IV (1951). At present, the author's *Japanese Music and Musical Instruments* (Tokyo & Rutland, Vermont: Tuttle, 1959) is the only general survey of all the major types of Japanese music, while his *Nagauta: The Heart of Kabuki Music* (Tokyo & Rutland, Vermont: Tuttle, 1963) is a detailed analysis of one theatrical genre. Robert Garfias provides a brief but scholarly survey of court dances in *Gagaku* (New York: Theatre Arts Books, 1959), while Elizabeth May has produced an informative study in *The Influence of the Meiji Period on Japanese Children's Music* (Berkeley: University of California Press, 1963). The ramifications of modernization in traditional music are discussed historically (not musically) in Komiya Toyotaka's *Japanese Music and Drama in the Meiji Era* (E. Seidensticker & D. Keene, translators) (Tokyo: Obunsha, 1956). The Columbia record *Japan, The Ryukyus, Formosa and Korea* (KL-214), compiled by Alan Lomax, is the only general collection available, though each country has an extensive LP record industry of its own. Folkways has produced *Korea* (FE 4424) and a fine set of Japanese folksong records (FE 4534). However, Folkways' *Buddhist Ritual Music* (FE 4449) is a paragon of misinformation. Lyrichord has released two interesting records of Buddhist music, primarily of the less developed Zen variety: *Japanese Temple Music* (LL 117) and *Zen, Goeika, and Shomyo Chant* (LL 116). Lyrichord also has issued *Gagaku* (LL 126), *Koto, Shamisen and Shakuhachi Music* (LL 131), *Japanese Kabuki Music* (LL 134), and *Japanese Noh Music* (LL 137), using musicians from Kyoto rather than Tokyo. The theatrical records are better than the instrumental, the *koto* performance being the most pedestrian. Kimio Eto has made several *koto* records on the World-Pacific label; these are somewhat affected by his long residence in America. The Caedmon record *The Noh* (TC 2019) is excellent and includes a text paraphrase. Columbia's *The Azuma Kabuki Musicians* (ML 4925) contains top performers playing in an overly resonant theatre. The second side includes two modern pieces, "Nagare" and "Ocho," complete with an electric bass *shamisen*. The best general collection from the standpoint of both repertoire and performer is the Ducretet-Thomson *Anthologie de la musique traditionnelle japonaise* (320 C 137-38). Nothing but the picture labels is wrong. The Musicaphon UNESCO series contains six volumes on Japanese music organized by genre (BM 30 L 2011, 12, 13, 14, 15, & 16). The Victor Company of Japan has provided English notes for its survey album, *The Traditional MUSIC OF JAPAN* (JL 32-4).

Index